THE COMMERCIAL ACTOR'S GUIDE

*All You Need to Start, Build,
and Maintain a Career*

Steve Carlson

HEINEMANN
Portsmouth, NH

Heinemann
A division of Reed Elsevier Inc.
361 Hanover Street
Portsmouth, NH 03801–3912
www.heinemanndrama.com

Offices and agents throughout the world

© 2005 by Steve Carlson

Library of Congress Cataloging-in-Publication Data
Carlson, Steve, 1943–
    The commercial actor's guide : all you need to start, build, and maintain a career / Steve Carlson.
        p. cm.
    ISBN 0-325-00824-8 (alk. paper)
    1. Television acting—Vocational guidance. 2. Television advertising—Vocational guidance. I. Title.
    PN1992.8.A3C284 2005
    791.4502'8'023—dc22   2005016345

Editor: Lisa A. Barnett
Production service: Aaron Downey, Matrix Productions Inc.
Production coordinator: Sonja S. Chapman
Cover design: Jenny Jensen Greenleaf
Compositor: Valerie Levy, Drawing Board Studios
Manufacturing: Jamie Carter

Printed in the United States of America on acid-free paper
09 08 07 06 05   VP   1   2   3   4   5

THE COMMERCIAL ACTOR'S GUIDE

DATE DUE

Charlotte J. Moeller

I wish you could have seen this but you saw everything
that led to it. We had a good ride, didn't we?
I love you, Mom.

CONTENTS

Introduction   ix

PART 1: THE ART OF THE AUDITION

CHAPTER 1:   The Business of the Business, Part 1   3

CHAPTER 2:   What's Your Type? And What To Do About It   13

CHAPTER 3:   Essentials   20

CHAPTER 4:   Professional Attitude   37

CHAPTER 5:   Competition   44

CHAPTER 6:   Preparation: The Actor   49

CHAPTER 7:   Preparation: The Copy   55

CHAPTER 8:   The Actual Audition   60

CHAPTER 9:   Direction   69

CHAPTER 10:   The Callback   73

PART 2: THE ART OF THE PERFORMANCE

CHAPTER 11:   The Concept and the Product   83

CHAPTER 12:   Rehearsal   88

CHAPTER 13:   Acting on the Set   95

CHAPTER 14:   The Director   99

CHAPTER 15:   The Spokesperson   104

CHAPTER 16:   Teleprompter and Cue Cards   108

CHAPTER 17:   Attitude on the Set   117

CHAPTER 18:   The Business of the Business, Part 2   121

CHAPTER 19:   Commercials: The First Step to Stardom   127

INTRODUCTION

THE ALLURE OF SHOW BUSINESS SEEMS TO HIT PEOPLE indiscriminately, regardless of race, creed, mental acumen, or social standing. It's an equal opportunity dream.

Although people who work in the performing arts are quite diverse, most of them share one common malady. Somewhere among the acting, singing, and dancing classes, they seem to have forgotten that *Show Business* is two words.

People will devote years of their time, money, and heart to perfecting the *show* part, not thinking at all about acting being a *business*. Most seem to figure that they'll either make it or they won't. If they don't, they'll park cars, wait tables, or tend bar until they do. If they do make it, they figure they'll be rich and famous and the money will simply take care of itself.

They're wrong about that.

In the first place, very few careers can be looked at in black or white. Very few people entering show business are going to be rich and famous, but very few will have no success at all. The vast majority of actors around the world do *some* work, get *some* success, and are constantly striving to get more of both.

Take it from one who's been doing it nearly forty years: the main constant in an actor's life is that of auditioning. Even if you've had great success in the past, today's producers and directors want to see what you can do *now*.

This makes it not only necessary to get to and stay at the top of your game, performance-wise, but also to handle your finances well, control your indebtedness, set up good business relations with your agents, casting directors, and every producer and director you meet, while making as comfortable and enjoyable a life as possible for you in the process.

That's what this book is about. Especially helpful, I think, is separating the skills necessary to successfully audition and get the role, and the skills necessary to effectively perform it on film. These are two very different tasks. Then, of course, there is dealing with it all as a *business*.

If you simply want to play and dabble in the industry and get the occasional commercial or day-player role, that's exactly what will happen to you. You get what you dwell on.

Don't be too surprised if you happen to notice one day that some of your peers who were taking the whole thing a bit more seriously are living and doing considerably better than you are. You both may have gotten what you went after. Aim high. It can be done. Having a successful and lucrative business in the film industry is difficult and the odds are against you, but it's still doable.

There's a sage old adage in acting that says, "The only thing you can bring to a role that no one else can bring is you." It's very true. I think that also applies to this book and me. My insights and observations are going to be a little different (sometimes a *lot* different) from other people's. But, after thirty-eight years of fooling them and getting away with it, there might be something here.

This business is filled with good-looking guys or girls who worked like crazy for a couple of years and were never heard from again. Part of the advice I can share is from the vantage point of a long career. Over the years, I've discovered many things that work—and many that don't.

I hope that reading this book and putting it to use will not only be an effective learning experience for you but an enjoyable one as well. It's a tough business, a trying business, and everybody doesn't win, but it's also not dental surgery. It's a fun business. Of course, much of the enjoyment depends on how you look at it. We'll even deal with that.

So, let's get on with it. Please enjoy, and . . .

Hope to see you on the set.
Steve Carlson

ONE

The Art of the Audition

1

The Business of the Business, Part 1

COMMERCIALS HAVE COME A LONG WAY. WHEN I FIRST STARTED acting professionally in the middle 1960s, I was under contract to Universal Studios. One of their stipulations was that while we were under contract, we could not do commercials. That was fine with us. We didn't want to.

A few years later, Universal started phasing out the contract program and most of us found ourselves out in the real world with no money, no job, and little promise of getting any.

This, I soon found out, is the limbo most actors live in daily. The exceptions are major, *major* stars (but even they have to be aware that what goes up can and will come down). Also exempt from this limbo, momentarily at least, are all actors during the run of their show, or series, film, or contract. All of which, unfortunately, do end.

For many of us, the problem of making a living and paying the bills suddenly loomed very large. Perhaps it is this reality of the business that turned people's perceptions of commercials around. Consider how times have changed:

Fifty years ago, most Broadway actors didn't even want to do movies. "Legitimate" actors considered film a bastardization.

Forty years ago, serious actors would deign to do movies but wouldn't stoop so low as to do television.

Thirty years ago, any actor would be pleased to do film or TV but would balk at doing commercials.

Twenty years ago, all actors would gladly work in all fields, but commercials were still a serious step down for a star.

Over the past ten years, it has been every man for himself!

Commercials represent some of the biggest money in this industry, and everyone from the newest neophyte to the most veteran of stars is pursuing the exposure and "big bucks" that this field offers.

Most people don't realize that many of our biggest stars—actors who still might not want to be associated with a product in the minds of American TV viewers—are representing companies commercially overseas. Huge (sometimes in the seven figures) sums of money are connected to these ventures, most of which are never seen in the USA.

A few years ago I was privy to a conversation that definitely got my attention. I was talking with my agent in LA when the phone rang. She answered it and was about to remind her secretary that she wanted all her calls held, but when she heard who was calling she excused herself from me for a moment and took the call. Her end of the conversation went something like this:

"Hello." Pause. "Yes. So that will be two million?" Pause. "Fine. We'll be in touch."

She hung up and resumed talking with me as though nothing had just happened. I wasn't quite ready yet.

"Wait a minute! Do you realize how long it's been since you made a two-million-dollar deal for me?" I kidded.

She gave me a droll look. "Darling, you're not Leonardo DiCaprio either."

So there you are. That was Japan calling. DiCaprio's commercial will never be seen in this country, and that's just fine with him. Not bad for a couple of days' work, eh?

If some of the announcers on commercials here in the US sound familiar, you are right again. New, extremely lucrative careers have been made behind the microphone by such stars as Martin Sheen, James Coburn, David Spade, Jack Lemmon, Sela Ward, James Garner, and many, many more.

One thing you really must remember, though, because it's very important: this is the *high* end.

The big-money acting group we were just discussing represents *less than half of one percent* of working actors!

I'm not going to bore you with stories about how tough this business is. You'd have to be living in a cave not to know that.

The point is that it's possible to succeed as an actor! Right? Of course it is. People are starting in this field all the time, and some of them are going to make it to the top. That's a fact! Why couldn't one of those people be you? Why not, indeed.

Commercials have launched many a career. Even though Tom Selleck had been working for years, his big break didn't come until he was seen nationwide in a Salem cigarette billboard. Diane Keaton was the toast of Broadway but first got film people's attention when she was wearing a track suit and talking about "fast banking" for a local LA bank. Meg Ryan and Jason Alexander had great commercial careers going before hitting it big (actually, Jason still does).

The realities of trying to make a living in this business are what attracted many of us to commercials. Let's take a look at the dollars and cents of it all.

Consider the following: As of 2005, the Screen Actor's Guild's daily rate for film and TV is $695.00.

I start with day players because no one is going to cast you in lead roles until they see what you can do. As you can see, you'd need a LOT of day player work to make a living.

Weekly scale for both is $2,411.00.

This is a little better, but remember that this number and all the others mentioned here are gross income. You will still have to deduct at least thirty-five percent for state and federal taxes and ten percent for your agent. (It would also be another ten or fifteen percent for a manager, but be very careful here. Managers are hardly ever necessary in the world of commercials.)

Guest Star, TV: (1/2 hour) $3,736 per week; (1 hour) $5,977 per week.

Congratulations! You've been doing good work and are being rewarded with a great guest star role in an hour show. Just think, if you were outrageously fortunate enough to get four of these in a year (pretty hard to get, especially at first) you would make a whopping $23,908—roughly what you could make working at McDonald's.

Of course, one of the things that makes show business so appealing is that once you start getting a name and a reputation, you can throw those numbers out the window and have your agents start negotiating your own personal fee. However, you have to get there first, and that usually entails making a living and paying the bills until the day Stardom comes calling.

Enter commercials. Let's take a look at these sets of numbers.

Daily Rate (Session Fee): $535.00.

Most commercials, by far, are shot in one day, occasionally two. Incidentally, this is the same fee for shooting a local, regional, or national spot. So far, we're still not at a living wage, but here comes the mother lode: residuals.

If you shoot a local or regional spot, all you'll get for the first thirteen weeks (quarterly payment) is your five-hundred-dollar session fee. If they run the spot for less than thirteen weeks, that's all you'll get. For each additional thirteen-week period that they run it or *intend* to run it, you'll get another five hundred dollars.

This is called a *holding fee*. What it does is keep the commercial alive so that the advertiser can run it any time they want to. It also keeps you *exclusive* to that product. You see, you can only do one type of commercial in a given field.

If you do a commercial for Coke, you cannot do a commercial for Pepsi until the Coke commercial is no longer active. This is referred to as a *conflict*. A commercial is in an active state as long as holding fees have been paid up to a certain date (whether they are running the spot or not). After that date, if they haven't renewed it, you are free to do anything. If they think they may run it in the future, the client may elect to keep paying holding fees in order to have that spot available for airing should they choose to do so.

This same rule also pertains if you, say, do a spot for a department store in Phoenix: as long as this commercial is still active you cannot do another commercial for a *different* department store in Phoenix. (You may, however, be able to shoot one for a different business in Phoenix that is not a conflict [for example, a tire store] or you could shoot a department store spot someplace else, like St. Louis.)

If you happen to shoot a spot that is to be used nationally, or in a large regional area, in addition to your holding fees you will also receive wild spot fees. They generally run another five hundred dollars, are paid every thirteen weeks, and enable the advertiser to use the spot as often as they want in a local or regional area.

Incidentally, your agent will keep track of the holding fee dates and check with the client when the time is up to make sure the commercial is indeed no longer active. If you don't have an agent, you'll have to do it yourself. When you first film the spot, mark down the dates and the name of the person to contact. (Then make sure you put the information where you won't forget about it.)

The *daddy of them all* is a national spot with a national run where your spot is run prime-time, coast to coast (such as on Monday Night Football, a first-run series, national news, etc.). These very lucrative spots pay you every time they are run.

Actually, the first time a commercial is run during each quarter, there is no residual fee. (The first time the commercial is run during the first quarter, the session fee covers it. In subsequent quarters, the holding fee covers the first run.) The second run is $122.70, and the third-run residual goes down to $97.35. Then it reaches a bottom figure of $46.65. You will be paid this amount each time the commercial is shown for the rest of the thirteen-week cycle.

The wonderful part of it all, though, is that at the beginning of the next thirteen-week cycle, the fees go back to the top figure, $535.00, and then the de-escalation process starts all over again.

If the spot runs for a while, or if the gods are smiling and you get more than one of these commercials running at the same time, suddenly you are making some money!

Because these spots are so expensive for the advertiser, there aren't as many nationals shot as the others, but they're still out there. It is still possible to get one.

You can see how having a few of these running could greatly help an actor's bottom line. Also, as in film and TV, the more work you do, the better known you will be in the business and the more opportunities you'll have to pass over *scale* and start negotiating *double scale* or even higher rates. That's possible, too.

Which brings us to my personal favorite aspect of this whole business: commercials are by far the most money paid for the least time expended. Many times you will shoot a spot that will continue to pay you for a year or two afterward, with no further involvement from you. Not bad, eh?

A wonderful case in point here is a Sure deodorant commercial that I shot a few years ago. All I had to do was putt, then raise my hand in victory and smile gleefully at my apparent success. ("Raise your hand if you're Sure.") Because of the camera angle, I didn't even have to make the putt.

We shot that little scenario to death, but it still took only a couple of hours. It then proceeded to run for more than three years—*nationally!* That's when you really love this business.

All right, so now we know why commercials are no longer dirty words. You are also getting a good look at why there is so much competition for each spot.

Remember, please, as in all of show business, "Many are called, few are chosen." When you consider the average yearly income for members of SAG is rumored to be less than $1,000.00, and when you think of all the people who are making millions, you can see there are a lot of actors making nearly nothing.

Where you are going to fall in this larger spectrum will depend upon how you approach and set up your particular business, and that's what it is: a *business*. If you still wonder about that, go back a page and look over those numbers again.

I can assure you that the actors I've been working with for the last few years, myself included, face it very much as a business, and if you wish to be competitive, you should too. Everything we'll be dealing with in this book will help you toward that end.

Commercials are also a great adjunct to a theatrical acting career because of the minimum time expenditure and the fact that you are using many of the same skills. We'll get into this subject in greater depth later, but right now just keep in mind that many an early acting career has been supported by commercials before the big break came. (Of course, these actors then come back to commercials to take advantage of their big name, but that's another story.)

Let's proceed with the building of career. (The words *career* and *business* will be used synonymously throughout this book because in this occupation, your career *is* your business.)

To begin with, you should give yourself every opportunity to succeed. By that I mean that you need to give yourself time to get established with a minimum of pressure.

The expression "keep the day job" basically means that you should not depend on making money from this field immediately. Careers are *built over time,* and people *become* established. It doesn't happen overnight, even though we would all like it to.

Along with having a source of finances to allow you enough time to get started, the correct mental attitude will help a lot. You're embarking on a new profession. You are going to be learning a great deal in the first few months. To make the most of this time, try to arrange your life so that you can devote the maximum attention to setting up your career. The best way to do that is to simplify as much as possible.

It's hard to concentrate on anything when you are plagued by debt, dealing with a difficult and demanding home life, or struggling to pay the rent each month.

Try to keep your monthly expenses at a manageable level. Having peace of mind gives you the freedom to *try* things, which is very important when starting an acting career.

You have to feel "free to fail." Otherwise, you'll be too needy to experiment. Sometimes the worst mistake you can make is to be afraid to make one. It's hard to think that way, though, if you're worried your babies won't get fed or you might get evicted from the house that you can't quite afford.

Simplify as much as you can at first, then let your life bloom and expand as your career and your experience grow.

ACTING IS ACTING

Many young actors view their acting career and doing commercials as two different things. It is true that you are usually dealing with different casting directors, and the audition process is somewhat different, but I think it's a mistake to totally separate them in your mind.

Acting in a commercial is still *acting*. The advertising copy is really a short script.

Unless you are the spokesman, very seldom will you actually be selling something. Usually, you will be *acting* as though you were in a certain life situation, i.e., having a headache or worrying because your car broke down, your dishes didn't get clean, or you need to buy a new vacuum cleaner. You are acting as though those things were really happening to you.

You will find that the better an actor you are, the better you'll do in commercials. Also, improvisational training is gold. Many times whole commercials are built around how people *react* to something. There may be little or no dialogue. The director will want to see a variety of reactions from you. The more comfortable and creative you can be with this process, the better your outcomes will be.

The primary task that actors face is to not look like they are acting. That's the case in commercials just as much as in film and TV.

FINDING AN AGENT

For those of you who are just starting out, you should know that the role of agents in the commercial business differs greatly from city to city. In Los Angeles, having an agent is mandatory and you can sign with only one at a time. In New York, agents are equally important but you may freelance with many. The first agent that calls you for the audition gets the commission if you get the job. As the time this book is being written, the New York system is in the process of evolving toward the Los Angeles system, so stay tuned on this one.

If you don't have many credits, you may find that getting an agent is one of the hardest things you've ever done. It can be extremely difficult and frustrating, but let's see how to take the sting out of it a little.

Realize, first, that the following views are mine. Others may disagree. Since there are no rules, this is quite a subjective area.

Unless you are outrageously fortunate, you will probably not be starting out with the biggest or best agency in town, but go for it anyway. Sometimes they like discovering an unknown. If you've got a look or a style that clicks with them, it may happen. Don't be dismayed if it doesn't.

You will usually have to start lower and work your way up. I've always thought a so-so agent was better than no agent. When you're starting out, you need work, experience, and exposure. Nearly any agent can get you started in that direction.

But how do you get the agent who is going to change the quality of life as you know it? Well, if you call them and tell them you are interested in representation, the secretary will tell you to send in a picture and résumé and if they're interested, they'll call you. She may also tell you that they are not taking on any new clients at that time.

That might not be the runaround it seems. Most good agencies run close to maximum. But she still asked you to send in your picture and résumé, didn't she? That's because no matter how full they are, an agent is always looking. You could have the exact look they're missing in the agency. If that's the case, I guarantee they'll find room for you. It never hurts to get your picture out.

If you ask agents how they like to get new clients, they'll say that they love it when someone in the business that the agent knows and respects (such as a director) has just worked with an actor they feel would be perfect for that agent and calls to let them know.

The ideal referral is a personal recommendation built on professional experience. You get that by working: doing commercials, industrials, student films, theater, all of it. Directors and producers work in all facets of the business, too. If you have a good work experience, let the director know you're in the market for an agent and see if he has any ideas.

The key is to get past the secretary, and personal recommendations of any kind will do that. If you don't have any connections, you will have to get some. Ask people.

Realize also that there are degrees of effectiveness in personal recommendations. When someone says, "Tell them I told you to call. Use my name," that's nice, but it's nicer if the person calls the agent himself, tells the agent about you, then has you call. That's guaranteed to set up a meeting.

The whole agent thing can be tough. There are no absolutes, but a few points should be kept in mind:

- Persevere. You may have to hang in there a bit before you see success.
- Get as much theatrical and film exposure as you can. Meeting and being seen by people in the industry is a must.
- Actively pursue personal recommendations. Ask. People can't help you if they don't know you're looking.
- When you do get a meeting with an agent, show the same degree of professionalism we'll be dealing with in this book: be confident, sure, capable. Remember that agents represent actors for a living. They have to feel they can develop interest in you, but they have to feel this interest themselves first.

In some smaller markets agents may not even be a factor and you'll find yourself dealing strictly with the casting directors. Learn what the reality of the business is in your market.

SHOULD YOU JOIN A UNION?

The importance of joining either or both of the acting unions, Screen Actors Guild (SAG) or American Federation of Television and Radio Artists (AFTRA), again depends upon your particular market. In larger cities and national markets, it is necessary to join both unions. In smaller markets or right-to-work states, it may not be that important. (We won't be dealing with the other acting union, Equity, because it deals strictly with live theater, not commercials.)

Whether you join or not, some of the union guidelines will benefit you anyway. For example, union rules stipulate that agents can legally take no more than ten percent of your gross. Managers generally take fifteen percent because they deal with far fewer people, but some agencies are now including the option to serve as managers also. That seems to be the case if you *really* want them to work for you. Check it out.

Your work hours, conditions, overtime pay, and turnaround time generally will also comply with SAG/AFTRA standards. (Turnaround time is the time between the hour you were released from work one day and the hour you are expected to show up at work the following day. Currently, the turnaround time for an actor is twelve hours, which means that if you were released from work today at 8:00 p.m., you could not be expected on the set tomorrow before 8:00 a.m.)

AFTRA has always been fairly easy to join. SAG has been the tough one. A "Catch-22" was involved in SAG for years. You couldn't work professionally unless you were a member of the Union, and you couldn't be a member of the Union unless you had worked professionally.

The only recourse was to have an established member sponsor you in. Today, the rules are different and make much more sense. Thanks to the Taft/Hartley Law, it's no longer necessary to be a member of a union before you can get your first job in the business, but you still have to work professionally before joining SAG. Taft/Hartley allows you to do that without penalty.

That first job can then be used as evidence that you have worked professionally in this business (definition: you have gotten paid for your services as a "principle player" rather than an extra) and are therefore qualified to join. You still have to come up with the money (this amount also varies according to market size), but at least, your technical requirements will be taken care of.

Before we begin analyzing various aspects of this business, here are a couple of thoughts I'd like to leave you with.

First of all, please know that you are going to be spending *much* more time auditioning than you are filming. To enjoy your life in this business, you must enjoy the process as much as possible.

Can you imagine if the only enjoyment a mountain climber got was when he reached the top? Considerably more time and effort is put into the climb than the brief moment spent on top. If the climber didn't enjoy the climb itself, he would probably never climb another mountain.

Of course, the top—in our case, the filming—is the payoff, the reward for work well done, but if you don't enjoy (or at least, not hate!) the time spent auditioning, you are probably getting into the wrong line of work.

Secondly, as we take a closer look at this whole process, it will be important to remember the "big picture." What is actually going on here? It's really quite simple. The point of auditioning, for the actor, right from the beginning, is to find out what the client is looking for and then convince them that you are the right person for the job. Period. No matter how involved or complicated things may seem at times, what we are trying to accomplish is simply that. Everything we'll be dealing with in this first part of the book is dedicated to bringing about that end.

2

What's Your Type?
And What to Do About It

BEFORE SERIOUSLY EMBARKING ON A COMMERCIAL ACTING career, you must first be very objective and brutally honest with yourself, about yourself. *You* are your product. You've got to know this product very well, professionally. You start by learning what the market is and how you fit into it.

At this point, even more important than knowing who you are is knowing how others perceive you. As actors, we're all dreamers, and I'm sure that you feel you could be a lot of things. For what we're talking about now, that is not the point.

What we're looking for here is what would be considered your *basic type*. If you are a fat person, it doesn't matter if you "feel" thin or are on a diet. Your basic character type (at this time, anyway) would be a fat person. You may be the coolest guy in the world, but if you look like a nerd (remember, be brutally honest now), then that would be your basic type.

Keep in mind that the people you're going to be dealing with in casting sessions don't know you and most of them never will, and it's not necessary. The people watching the TV spots you've filmed won't know you either. What's important is how you are perceived.

In a thirty- or sixty-second commercial, the actor may be on screen a fraction of that time, so if the client wants to make a statement about what kind of person, family, or business uses their product, they have to do it immediately and with as few words as possible.

That's actually one of the main reasons they use people in their commercials at all—to make the statement that "This is the type of person who uses *Our Product."* To begin with, for casting purposes, let's go beyond your type. What we need first is your *stereotype!*

Initial instructions for commercial castings are done in stereotypes or generalities. Let's say they want a clean-cut teenager, a doctor, the mother of an infant, and a truck driver. From all the commercials you've seen in your life, reading over that list brings images to your mind in each case—that's what we're talking about. Those images are the stereotypes. What category would you fall into?

The man who gets the job as the doctor may in actuality be a truck driver, but if he looks like what we generally think of as a doctor, very seldom will he be cast as a truck driver.

The main categories we will be dealing with are teenagers (ingénues, young leading men, and characters), Moms and Dads (young and middle-aged, leading actors, and characters), business professionals (all ages, straight and character), and grandparents. (*Note:* Most categories contain the subcategory of *character.* Most comedians fall under this heading, but so do what are sometimes referred to as "real people.")

Stereotypically speaking, knowing what you are sets up what you could be. There are plenty of crossovers—but within reason. Our middle-aged Dad could probably also be an airline pilot, a CEO, fishing partner with some business buddies, spokesman for Advil, etc. Our young character Mom could also be a sales clerk, a businessperson, a bank teller, spokesperson for a line of toys, and a number of other things.

There is work to be had in all categories. As a current or future professional in this business, it is imperative that you know your niche. It's unprofessional and embarrassing for everybody when the 30-year-old ex-model still tries to compete with the 20-year-old hard-bodies like he used to. You have to know who and what you are *today.*

If they need a "stunner" in a bikini, you'd be amazed at the number of beauties they have to choose from. If they need a weight lifter, they'll find one.

If they need a loving family, they'll pick a Mom and Dad who seem to fit together and who look like they would be loving parents. These two people may not even know each other, but it doesn't matter. What matters is that they look the part and can give the necessary feel to the spot.

Looking at themselves honestly is not something most people, even actors, readily do. They have their self-image, and for better or worse, they feel they are stuck with it. ("That's just the way I am.")

This can go either way. Some people feel they are better, prettier, and smarter than they really are, but most of the time it's the other way around. Insecurity and self-doubt are very well known in our society—

especially, it seems, in those who are sensitive enough to seek careers in the performing arts.

Either way will kill you, and not just in the obvious ways. Of course there's the embarrassment of trying out for something you're totally wrong for (your agent should help here, though) but what about something that others think you're right for but you don't? For example, you might find yourself protesting, "I'm just not the 'Hero' type" or "No guy that handsome would ever fall for *me*. I'd never be able to pull it off," and so on.

By the way these people are perceived by others, they may fit this role perfectly, but their limiting self-images have knocked them out of the running. Ninety-nine percent of the time their self-doubts and insecurities will shine through their audition and ruin any chance they may have had.

That's why it's important to look at yourself through the eyes of your category.

All right. Now that you're established in a *type*, it's time to get creative. We know basically what kind of person you are perceived to be, and now's the time to explore what kind of person you could be (categorically speaking).

Every girl that gets the guy is not gorgeous. Not every hero looks like Brad Pitt. That is the stereotype, however, and most of the time commercial casting will go in that direction. But not always! Be flexible.

The only thing that is certain in this business is that nothing is certain. Be honest with yourself, but don't unduly limit yourself. These are not conflicting statements.

As I mentioned before, the main reason people are hired for commercials is to help create an image of what type of person uses a particular product. (Otherwise they'd just show the product and have the announcer talk about it. Much cheaper.) Some clients take it so seriously they may act like they're casting *Gone with the Wind* instead of a local spot for Carlson's BBQ Sauce, but the client needs to find an actor he's comfortable with because his product is going to be identified with that actor.

If you get the job, as long as that commercial is running, your likeness and image will be linked to that product. There is an automatic identification factor when people watch television. The clients are not only aware of that, but they count on it.

You were probably hired for one or both of the following reasons: to appeal to people who are like you or who want to be like you, either physically (being handsome, healthy, and happy) or by circumstance (taking a Princess Cruise, driving a Cadillac, or having a baby without diaper rash).

The first part of this book deals with how to get the job. You don't want to walk away from the audition with excuses, you want to walk away with the job. The first step in doing that is to understand as fully as possible what the clients are looking for. The more you understand what they are looking for, and why, the more you will be able to give it to them. Understanding the process and your place in it can help greatly.

Another reason self-knowledge is so important in film is that, unlike theater, the film character is practically always *you*, especially when it comes to commercial characters.

In theater, a thin, twenty-five-year-old man could be cast as Falstaff, and with the right makeup and wardrobe, pull it off. On film, they would simply hire a heavy fifty-year-old. The camera is just too close, too intimate to get away with something like that easily. (It still is possible, of course. It's just much more difficult.)

No, you can count the fact that any commercial character you play will not be far away from the real you. Rather than looking outside to build a character, it will all be internal.

"How would I feel if I won the Lottery?" "How would I feel if my daughter was getting married?" "How would I let my wife know that this is the worst tuna casserole in the world and oh, how I wish she would try such-and-such a brand?"

YOUR STRONG POINTS

While we're dealing with self-analysis, you need to be able to identify your strong points. In other words, why would anyone cast you?

A good place to start in determining this is to ask yourself what made you think you'd be able to do commercials in the first place. You wouldn't be reading this book unless somewhere along the line you had decided that you'd be right for them. What was it? The way you look? Your acting ability? Your sense of humor? Other talents that you think would be appropriate?

Answer those questions and you'll be on your way to knowing what it is that you've got to sell. These are weapons in your arsenal. The more things you can do, the more things you know, the more capable and well rounded a person you are, the better off you will be. They are also great confidence builders.

Identifying your basic type and specific attributes is the first step in positioning yourself in this business. Regardless of type, there is no shortage of competition. People in this business are good—very good. If you are going to compete professionally with them, you'll have to be as good or better than they are. Don't think you're going to step into this business and start out-acting people. That just won't happen. Being a good actor is a given. You have to be good to even play this game.

Remember always that the intent of the commercial is to introduce or remind the public of this particular product and to make them want to buy or experience it—it's as simple as that. Try not to overcomplicate the situation.

The feel of the commercial and the image it conveys are of supreme importance. This business is no place for an actor's attitude. This is the time and place to present yourself as the nicest person in the world.

The reason you're there is to have people identify with you, listen to what you have to say, and emulate what you are doing. People don't identify with people they don't like or respect; conversely, people have a tendency to trust a nice person more than someone who is not. Do you see a pattern here?

BEING THE ROLE

Over the years, both in commercials and television, I've been in the position of being hired first, then participating in the hiring of a woman who would fit well with me. The best way to do that, of course, was for me to be present at the audition. Not many actors get a chance to see the audition process from the other side of the desk. I found it very interesting.

One of the first things I noticed was that I could usually tell within the first ten seconds whether this actress was right for what we needed or not. At first I felt terrible, like I wasn't giving them a chance, but I discussed this with other casting directors and they admitted that it happens to them, too.

The lesson here, then, is to make the most of those initial ten seconds. What that means is that you need to walk into the audition room *as the character* you are trying out for. You don't have to impress them with what a good actor you are. The clients want people to get a glimpse of you and get the feeling they want conveyed. The best way you can show them that you can do it is to *do it*. Do it to them! If you sell *them*, you've got the part.

To pull this off, you've got to have confidence in yourself as this character. Most commercial situations involve a slice of life: having coffee, going shopping, buying a new car (or suit, or basketball, or antacid, etc.). Even if it's a far-out situation, put yourself into it. How would you feel if you were on a safari in Africa? Or what if your bathroom drain started talking to you, telling you that it has big problems? Walk into the room full of that feeling.

But it has to feel right to you before it can appear right to them. (And you thought you didn't need to act to do commercials. Ha!)

DRESSING FOR THE PART

Actors often wonder how far to go in dressing for the part. The answer is an individual one. It's totally up to you, but common sense does figure in here.

If the call is for a man in a business suit, I would go out on a limb and say that if you've got a business suit and you want this job, wear it. Some actors get pretty casual in LA after a while. They realize that nine times out of ten, for spokesmen situations, they only shoot you from the waist up. So, some show up in shorts, with a shirt, tie, and sport coat. Of course, if the casting director happens to want a wide shot, or the clients themselves happen to show up that day, this actor just lost the job.

Following the logic I just mentioned about being the part when you walk into the room, certainly *looking* the role is a large part of that. Actually, dressing like what or who you are supposed to be is a great help in getting into the character, so don't think of it as a problem or a drag. Think of it as one more thing you can do to transform yourself into the character.

I've seen people show up for auditions in full ski apparel, full flame-retardant racing gear, tuxedos, and on and on. It can be effective. Not only does it show that you can look the part, but it might also convey that you have some experience in that area. (Why else would you have ski clothes if you didn't ski?)

I'm going to borrow a story from my first book, *Hitting Your Mark*, because it makes a good point here.

"The farthest I saw an actor go in this regard, was for an audition in which they needed old, grizzled cowboys. The waiting room was filled with old, grizzled cowboy actors. Any one of them could have done the role. One particular actor was getting kidded pretty strongly by his co-actors.

"I didn't know why until he was called in. He got up, picked up the SADDLE he had brought with him, threw it over his shoulder and walked in. Everybody cracked up. Talk about overkill.

"However, a couple of months later, I saw the spot on the air and there was the guy with the saddle, playing the old, grizzled cowboy. He had taken a chance and it paid off."

This is also the time to watch little things like your posture. Slumping into the room is not going to get anyone's attention unless your character slumps. If so, slump away! If not, straighten up as your character would. Look them in the eyes (or not) as your character would, then do the audition scene as the character would.

BE YOURSELF

(Is this a contradiction? No.)

This always used to be a tough one for me. I'm an actor (and a Gemini). I can be all sorts of people. Which one do you want? I can be nice, I can be strong, I can be gregarious or sullen, funny or quiet, on and on, and all are me. Well, parts of me. I was missing the point.

Going back to our *basic type*, if we keep in mind what the character is supposed to be (say, a businessperson), and I'm asking the question, "How would I feel or act if I were a businessperson in this situation?" the answer to that question tells me what I need to know.

"What would I do if . . . ?" Answer that question, feel it, and do it. That's bringing *you* into the part.

If you're still having trouble nailing which *you* to bring to the audition, bring the one you don't have to think about.

WATCHING TV FOR FUN AND PROFIT

The commercials on television provide a perfect training ground for the commercial actor—because there are so bloody many of them! Seriously, put down the remote control and stop muting the commercials, Don't zip past commercials on shows you've taped, and keep a sharp eye out for other actors who are your type.

These actors are your competition, and you've got an opportunity to analyze what they are doing. Why did they get this job? What do you suppose the client saw in these actors that made them want to hire them? If they work a lot, what is the recurring theme that they bring to everything they do? Visualize yourself in their spots, too. Could you have done them as well as they did? Would you have? If not, what would you have to do or learn in order to do it as well—or better?

Here's a great opportunity to study their tricks. Find out what's working for them, then perhaps adapt their techniques to fit your particular personality. Watch, learn, and study. Find out what makes them good. Then blend those attributes with your own and see what happens.

The results may be very interesting. We learn from others unconsciously all the time. What you're doing here is simply doing it consciously.

3

Essentials

PICTURES

The actor's primary contact with the show business world is, of course, his picture. As such, care should be given that you are representing yourself correctly. This is not an area to be taken lightly.

Realize that casting directors (depending on the size of their market) can receive hundreds of submissions a day. Just imagine the speed with which they leaf through the pile of that day's pictures. And now that so much casting is being done on the Internet and it has become so simple to submit digital files, there are even *more* pictures!

If you don't have a shot that's a good, current one that *says something*, odds are you are going to end up in the large stack being thrown out, instead of the small stack of people being asked in to audition.

In big cities, the scenes are very much like I just mentioned. In smaller markets there certainly won't be the crush of numbers, but you still have to get their attention. Many times casting directors will show clients pictures of actors that they've accumulated before any actual casting starts. The client chooses which people they would like to see—another case for being represented by the best picture you can put out there.

Choosing a Photographer

There are a number of things to keep in mind when selecting a picture. The first is to find a photographer who specializes in head shots. In smaller markets this might be difficult, but medium to large markets will include many who do this sort of thing as a specialty. Check them out.

Perhaps your agent or a fellow actor could recommend a couple of photographers. Also, if you love another actor's head shots, don't be shy about asking who took them. You don't even have to know them. Most actors will be flattered that you like their shots enough to ask and will gladly tell you.

When you have a couple of photographers to check into, make an appointment to see their "books." This is a cross-section of the type of work they do, and all professional photographers will have one. (Please don't have your brother-in-law take them. They always end up looking like your brother-in-law took them.)

Since you know and are now comfortable with your type, ask how the photographer sees you. Make sure the two of you agree. Tell him what you had in mind and ask him what he would suggest. You need someone who sees you the way you want to be seen—the way you and your agent agree is your best professional image.

If possible, it's good to have your agent involved in this process right from the beginning. Since these pictures are going to be their tools for trying to sell you (which is also the way they make their living, remember), they have to be just as comfortable and feel just as good about them as you do. If you don't have an agent, by the way, your pictures may be instrumental in helping you get one.

When you find someone who is easy to talk with and be around, someone who seems to hear what you are saying, someone whose body of work shows that he is capable of doing what he says, this could be your photographer.

Keeping Up with Trends

One of the most important things to be aware of in this business is to *get and stay current*. As we will be discussing later, this includes everything from hairstyle to wardrobe and, in some cases, even style of delivery! It's especially important to keep your pictures current. Let's look at some options.

The Composite This used to be the standard for anyone in commercials. As of this writing, it has been replaced in the LA and NY markets by a simple head shot, but in other parts of the country people still prefer a composite.

What's important is to see and know your particular market. If you live in Columbus, Ohio, it doesn't really matter what people are doing in LA. What matters is what is preferred in Columbus. That's where you are trying to get work.

A composite is actually a better representative of the actor. It consists of a full head shot on the front and a collection of other poses, usually three, on the other side plus personal stats and information about the actor.

This format allows an actor to explore his category pretty well. One of my earlier composites showed a smiling head shot on the front. On the back I had a young Dad playing with his (my) son, a businessman in a suit in an office, and a rugged shot (flannel shirt, etc.) out camping, which covered my main stereotyped categories.

If you are putting together a composite, make sure you use images in your category for which you would realistically be cast and for which there is a current market. (You may look like a great sheik, but how many commercial roles do you think there'll be for it? You're right. None.)

That's another good reason for using a photographer who is familiar with this type of shooting. You can get some very good suggestions from them.

The Head Shot This is currently the most popular form of picture in commercial use today. Since it doesn't encompass the variation a composite does, you have to hit pretty much in the middle. Here you aim for a shot that is as representative of you and your category as possible. Keep it light. Very seldom will there be a dark, brooding commercial. (If there is, use your theatrical picture.) Commercial shots are friendly, easy, and approachable.

Keep the background simple, and always be alone. This is not the spot for that cute two shot.

"How about if I have a number of different head shots for different roles, like a housewife, a businesswoman, a mom, and maybe one out fishing?" I can hear you asking. Good question. And in the best of all possible worlds, that's exactly what you should have. However, if you happen to be in a medium to large market, it's doubtful the agents will spend the time going over all the pictures that you have on file to find the very best one for that particular job.

If you are in a smaller market or have an agent that will actually do that, go for it. But once again, you must see what the fact of the matter *is*, not how you would like it to be.

Remember also that anyone can say anything. Years ago I presented my agents with three different types of head shots. I didn't think that was too many, and they seemed pleased and assured me that they would send out the proper picture for each role.

Months later I happened to see the picture they'd sent in for a businessman role, and it was a *rugged, outdoors* picture! When I inquired at the agency I discovered that they had just put all my pictures in a stack

Steve Carlson

Figure 3-1a: Four examples of head shots.

and hadn't even mentioned to the girl that actually did the picture pulling that she should try to find the picture that was most appropriate for the role. (She was so frantically busy that I don't know if she could have done it, anyway.)

The outdoors pictures were on the top, so the first twenty-five people who wanted to see me would get an outdoors picture, regardless of the spot. The next twenty-five would get a businessman picture, and so on.

My point in sharing this story is that you need to follow up on how your pictures are being sent. If a situation like mine is occurring, just give them a good, representative head shot and let it go at that.

Rita Kinsey

Figure 3-1b

Actually, there is a good use for those other shots. When you go on a call, you always take a picture and a résumé, right? (The answer to that question is, "Right!") You would take the outdoor picture to the outdoor audition, the businessperson shot to the businessperson audition, and so on. There's no rule that says you have to take the same picture that was submitted originally.

Don't try to cover your category by giving the casting director more than one picture unless they request it. Most feel they have too many pictures around anyway. The additional ones you have encumbered

BARBIE CHAMPION

Figure 3-1c

them with will not be appreciated. They'll be thrown away immediately. It's just a waste of money.

Here are some general rules for getting the most effective head shot. You already know your type, so you know approximately what kind of shots you are going to need. You have found a photographer who specializes in (or at least does a lot of) commercial head shots.

The actual session is usually preceded by a meeting with the photographer a day or two beforehand so you can discuss what you want. He will get in mind what locations would be good for you, and he will

MARK RUBALD

Figure 3-1d

advise you what to wear and suggest a change of clothing or two to bring along, for different looks.

Incidentally, location shooting is best for commercial head shots. What you're selling is "naturalness," and outside light gives that look. Plus, you want to look like a "real person," not a model. Being out in a setting of any kind helps create that feeling. You don't actually have to be outside, but preferably not in a studio. An office, a kitchen, a restaurant . . . you know, real places. Just make sure the background is not busy. You don't want to have to fight the background for attention in the shot.

Be sure that the pictures you are taking are of *you*, not a character. Don't try to *be* anyone but yourself (and your type) in these shots. Remember how many pictures the casting people are dealing with. They do not have the time to figure out what you were trying to do or who you were trying to be in the shot. Keep it simple, relaxed, and easy.

Make sure you come across as likable. Remember, you want to be identified with a client's product. They have to like you in order for them to think that the audience will like you. Keep that in mind through your various poses.

Later in the book we'll go into the importance of *acting through your eyes*. That should be done as you pose for your pictures also. That is the first place someone looks when viewing a head shot. If anything is going on in the picture, it'll be going on in your eyes.

Thoughts show through the eyes. One effective trick is to have a secret. Toy with the camera a little. You know something it would love to know, but you are not going to tell it now . . . maybe later . . . maybe not.

Also, try not to pose. Keep the shots as candid as possible. Casting directors and clients want *real, likable* people, like you. These pictures should show them how real, likable, easy, and honest you can be.

One of the realities you have to deal with is that there are hundreds, if not thousands, of actors around. Yes, we want you to be special and to stand out, but requiring more work of agents or casting directors is not the way to do it.

Styles come and go. The types of pictures preferred by casting directors and agents also differ in various parts of the country. You're going to have to do your own research to find out what the current preferences are. The best way to do this is to ask your agent or the casting directors. Have them show you an example from someone who is working a lot, or if you have friends who are working more than you are, take a look at their pictures. Is there anything that you can learn from them? If something is working for them, perhaps it will work for you, too.

There are even trends that exist down to the type of picture. A few years ago, the 3/4 shot was in. I heard one casting director say that if the actor's shot wasn't a 3/4 she couldn't really trust it because she didn't know how old it was. Since the 3/4 was a recent trend, if you had one, she would know the picture wasn't more than a year or two old.

The current trend at the time of this writing is the basic head shot, but by the time you read this, who knows? Sometimes there are even preferences as to whether or not the picture should have a border, whether it should be a glossy or matte finish, whether you should have your name and agent on the front, and so on.

Figure 3-2a: Examples of 3/4 shots.

Before you invest your money, make sure you are in accordance with the accepted professional standards for your market.

Color

Color pictures used to be so expensive that they were used strictly by models and well-heeled young actors who were trying to impress. It didn't work, because they were just too ostentatious.

Michelle Post

Figure 3-2b

Today, however, we have a new ball game. With digital photography, it is now outrageously cheap to reproduce color and since so many casting submissions are being done via the Internet, hundreds of copies are no longer needed.

As a result, in major markets practically every actor has at least one color shot in his arsenal. As with everything we deal with, check to see what's preferred in your market, but I wouldn't be surprised if you ended up with some color shots in there somewhere.

RÉSUMÉS

Technically, résumés are not all that important for commercial work because you never list the commercials you've done anyway. (If that Ford commercial that you did two years ago has been off the air for a year, it's not a conflict for anything. But if you've got it on your résumé, the people at Chevrolet won't even bother to see you.)

For commercials, résumés are strictly for impressing. Hardly anybody wants to hire someone for their first job. If they're hiring someone to represent their product, they're going to want to be certain that this person can handle it and do a good job, and not just in the audition room, but on the set as well, when it all counts. Résumés can do that for you.

Résumés list your body of work (theatrical, film), stats, experience, training, agents, unions, and skills. If you have done movies, list them. If you have done TV episodes of any sort, list them. If you have done theatrical productions of any note, list them.

If you've got a body of work behind you, creating an impressive résumé is no problem. But what if you haven't? Well, then you need to get creative. If you are planning on becoming a professional in this field, then you surely must have done at least some stage work to let you get the idea that you may have the ability in the first place. (If you haven't, I admire your chutzpah but I suggest you get to work and get some experience.)

List that stage work. If you have to go back to your high school, college, or little theater productions, do it. If the résumé still looks pretty empty, list the various places you've studied, any commercial acting workshops you may have attended, cold reading classes, anything that will show that you are prepared, trained, and capable of handling their commercial.

If you've done a lot of work, list your best work and your best roles. If you or anything you've ever done have received any awards or any specific acclaim, by all means, list them, too. This is your chance to blow your own horn. Your picture comes first, and your résumé is the second step in making yourself special. If you have anything that you can talk

JANA WILSON

Hair: Black	Height: 5'6"	(*space for Agent's logo*)
Eyes: Brown	Weight: 125 lbs.	

THEATER

P.S. Your Cat is Dead	Chris	Arvada Playhouse
Lend Me a Tenor	Maria	Ohio State University
Summer Stock Co.	Various roles	Ohio State University

TELEVISION

Unsolved Mysteries	Kate	Cosgrove Meurer Prods.

MOTION PICTURES

Promise Keepers	Receptionist	INS Productions

– Commercials: Upon Request –

TRAINING

Theater Arts Major / 3 years
Ohio State University

Barbara Rice Stone (acting coach) – 1 year

Workshops:

Tony Barr
Mike Fenton

SPECIAL SKILLS

Swimming, diving, aerobics, jazz dancing, tennis (really good!!), skiing, horseback riding (western)

Figure 3-3a: Two résumés.

STEVE   CARLSON

Ht: 6'   Wt: 175

Hair: blond   Eyes: blue

SAG/AFTRA   **video tape available**

__MOTION PICTURES__   (Partial Listing)

THE YOUNG WARRIORS	STARRING	Universal
THE BROTHERS O'TOOLE	STARRING	Independent
LEGAL ALIENS	STARRING	Independent
DEADLIER THAN THE MALE	STARRING	J. Arthur Rank (Int.)
SHADOW FORCE	CO-STARRING	Independent

__TELEVISION SERIES__   (Contract Roles)

GENERAL HOSPITAL	Dr. Gary Lansing	(4 years) ABC
THE YOUNG & THE RESTLESS	Mark Henderson	(3 years) CBS
THE BOLD & THE BEAUTIFUL	Dr. Tim Madigan	(reoccurring 3 yrs.) CBS
A NEW DAY IN EDEN	Josh Collier	(1 year) SHOWTIME
YOU BET YOUR LIFE	co-host with Richard Dawson	NBC (pilot)

__OTHER TELEVISION__   (Over 50 episodes - Partial Listing)

SEINFELD (FINAL EPISODE)	GUEST STAR	Castle Rock/NBC
BAYWATCH	GUEST STAR	Baywatch Prods.
DICK CLARK'S ROCK & ROLL ERA	HOST	Time/Life
REAL TV (Pilot)	HOST	Paramount
THIS IS THE LIFE	GUEST STAR	Family Prods.

("ALL THE DAYS OF MY LIFE" **Emmy award winner**, 1988)

CRAZY LIKE A FOX	GUEST STAR	Columbia
MICKEY SPILLAINE'S MIKE HAMMER	GUEST STAR	Columbia

__AUTHOR__

HITTING YOUR MARK: *What Every Actor Really Needs to Know on a Hollywood Set*   Published by Michael Wiese Prod., 1999

THE COMMERCIAL ACTOR'S GUIDE: *All You Need to Start, Build, and Maintain a Career*   Published by Heinemann   2005

HITTING YOUR MARK   Special 2nd Edition

__SPECIAL SKILLS:__ Singing, guitar (6 & 12), motorcycles, skiing, glider pilot, tournament tennis, golf, horseback riding, all sports

Figure 3-3b

about that makes you stand out from the rest, here's the place for it. You do have to use your head here, however.

If you're thirty you might not need to list anymore that you were High School Homecoming Queen, but you still might want to let them know that you were Miss Nebraska. Being a champion bull rider or skier or most anything like that should be included.

We'll talk about a little device called the *ear* (or the *bug*) later, but if you are adept at using one, that's a good thing to list on your résumé also.

Important: Do not list things you didn't do, and do not list things that you *can't* do. You *will* get caught, and it *will* be embarrassing, and you will totally lose credibility with whoever caught you, and you will never work for them again!

I've never lied on a résumé in my life, but I found out how it would make you feel if you got caught anyway.

I'm a good skier. Years ago I was auditioning for a Scope commercial that required an actor to ski into the spot before the dialogue. Only good skiers were supposed to audition. (Of course, they had to take our word for it.)

By the callback they were worried. They kept asking us, "Are you *really* a good skier? *Really?*" The other actors and I assured them that we were. Well, I got the job, and a day or two later we met at four in the morning and made the trek up to a local Southern California ski area.

Two problems came into play. The first was the fact that at six in the morning, when we got there, the slopes were solid ice. The second problem was that the director had never skied in his life and knew nothing about it.

Once we got settled, he asked me to go up and show him how good a skier I was. (No pressure, though. Right?) Confident as I am of my skiing ability, I did mention to him about the ice. He didn't want to hear it. As far as he was concerned, either I could ski or I couldn't.

Well (you can see this coming), I rode up to the top, came down, did two lovely turns, lost an edge and slid on my backside all the way down this little mountain, depositing myself at the director's feet. He yelled, "*(Expletive deleted)!*" and stormed away. I felt terrible.

He set up the shot so I would only have to ski three feet into it. I guess he figured that even I could handle that. I was outrageously frustrated for the next couple hours until the sun came out and softened the ice to the extent that it became ski-able. I could hardly wait to get back up the mountain to show the director that I was, in fact, a skier, which I did. Repeatedly! I made sure he saw me. We also talked about it.

I explained the way snow and ice worked, and he explained that he didn't know anything about skiing but, yes, he could see that I could, in fact, ski but now he was also happy with the way he'd set up the commercial, so he didn't change it. At least I went home with my integrity intact. (It was also a very successful national commercial that ran about two years.)

Bottom line: Don't lie. If you don't have enough experience in anything to fill up a résumé, don't use one at all. The purpose of a résumé is to point out the things you've done, not to embarrass you. Besides, as I mentioned, they're not that important in commercials anyway.

Conflicts

We mentioned conflicts earlier. Remember that a commercial doesn't have to be on the air to be active. If holding fees have been paid to a certain date, the commercial is active to that date.

But even if your commercial for a given product has been off the air for a while, the client may still balk at seeing you. (Remember the identification we were talking about? If the client feels there is any chance in the world that people may look at you and remember the Sony commercial you did, they won't hire you for RCA.)

The way to solve this potential problem on your résumé is to use the catch phrase "Commercials upon Request." If they ask, tell them, but if there are no current conflicts, there's no law that says you have to tell them about the commercial you did for their competition two years ago. If there's not currently a conflict, there's no reason to even mention it. (They hardly ever ask, by the way. They're concerned with conflicts. That's all. If it's not a conflict, they don't care about it, and conflicts are strictly commercials that are active *now.)*

If you haven't done any commercials or perhaps have done only one, I wouldn't mention commercials at all on the résumé. If you've done at least two, use the catch phrase.

On the off chance that you're thinking of doing something that would be a conflict anyway, let me caution you against that. The Screen Actors Guild and AFTRA monitor airplay closely for residual purposes. Records exist. The client doesn't have to physically see the conflicting commercial for you to get caught.

If you do get caught, the retributive action is for the guilty party to pay to have the spot re-shot with another actor. Do you have any idea how much one of those spots cost?

Answer: More than enough to make you never want to test this rule.

Printing

Some actors have their résumés printed on the back of their pictures. Actually, it looks rather classy, but it doesn't make a lot of sense to me. Every time you get a new job, you will have to throw out your pictures and order a new batch. If you're planning on working a lot, I'd stick to stapling your résumé to the back of the picture. It's not only cost effective but it works just fine.

The Point of Having a Résumé

Just in case you're getting caught up in all the minutiae regarding résumés, it's good to step back and focus on what you are actually trying to accomplish here. What's the point?

Your résumé should be compiled to accomplish two goals: To make the reader confident that you can handle their job, and to make them to want to meet you. Period.

If your résumé does that, you've got a good one.

WARDROBE

Commercial wardrobe is primarily common sense. This is another place where it's necessary to know your type. By seeing others of your type on TV, you can get a good idea of what you will be auditioning for and how to dress accordingly.

In your closet, clean and ready to be worn, should be at least one outfit for you to wear that is casual, a business suit, something of an upscale nature like a dress suit or gown, and if you happen to be a babe or a hunk you should also have a swim suit and/or a shorts outfit ready.

Since most of us are dealing with budgets, realize that you don't have to go crazy here. (You really don't need to keep a saddle handy.) What you need to do on an audition is give the client an idea of how you would look in their commercial. If you get it, their wardrobe department will supply the Armani suit for you to wear. Auditioning in the fifty-dollar suit from J.C. Penney will do just fine.

Incidentally, if you are new to the business, know that once you get the commercial, you will have a wardrobe call. They will usually ask you to bring a selection of outfits from your own closet that may work for what they are doing.

Let's say it's a camping spot. Your good ol' worn Levis will probably look a lot more natural on you than the jeans that they bought that afternoon. Same with good ol' plaid shirt, etc. The wardrobe person will also have a selection, usually a large one, from which they normally choose. But it is standard practice for them to ask you to bring your own clothes as well.

I remember a wardrobe call I got for one of my first commercials when I was just getting started years ago. They asked me to bring a "selection of business suits," and I laughed as I went off to the call in my one and only sport coat. That was as close as I could get at the time, and it was just fine. You do what you can. No one can ask any more of you than that.

Not only will they pay you for wearing your own clothes if they choose from your wardrobe, but you can usually buy the clothes they brought for half price! The production company can only deduct fifty percent of their wardrobe cost, so if they can pick up the other fifty percent by selling them to you, why not? Many times they can and do. (I must admit that a good part of my personal wardrobe over the years came from various shoots.)

Don't make the mistake of thinking that how you dress isn't all that important. You might wonder how necessary it is to put on a suit to go to an audition. They certainly know that you *can* wear a suit. "Don't they have any imagination at all?"

Well, many don't. Even those who do don't like using it very much. They would rather have what they are looking for standing in front of them, than to try to imagine whether you could, maybe, be that person.

What it could come down to is this: the audition is for the role of a businessman. You and another actor are both perfect for the spot. You both look the part and did a good job with the audition. He is wearing a business suit and you aren't. The tie is broken. He gets the job. They don't have to use their imagination with him. With you, they do. You made them work harder.

When you walk in the door for the first audition, you want to *be* the character so much that they could just shoot your audition and put it on the air. Correct wardrobe goes a long way toward creating that feeling.

Remember how important those first few seconds are. To borrow an advertising line that fits perfectly here, "You never get a second chance to make a first impression."

CHAPTER

4

Professional Attitude

EARLIER I MENTIONED THAT YOU HAD TO BE A GOOD ACTOR TO even play this game, and it's true. Professional competition is not like trying out for the junior class play, where the outcome was very simple: the best actor in school got the lead. Well, your competition out there— all of us—are the ones who got those leads, probably, just like you did.

The point I'm trying to make here is that acting talent alone won't make it in this market. If everyone is such a good actor, you might be wondering, what is the competition based on? Well, in the next chapter we'll take an in-depth look at the process of competition, but for now, we'll look at the first part of the answer to that question: the people who succeed in this business have a good, solid, professional attitude (and I consider this topic important enough to devote, not one, but two chapters to it).

Here, we're not so concerned with how much talent you have, but *how you use it*. How do you present yourself? As a professional actor, you should have a positive aura of ability, strength, and confidence surrounding you in any audition or performance situation. If you don't have those qualities, there are ways to get them.

BEING HEALTHY

We'll start with generalities before getting specific. The absolute first thing to be concerned with is being and looking healthy. Your mind and body are your instruments as well as your product. Your image and abilities are what you are selling. Regardless of your type, no client is going to want to associate his product with someone who doesn't act or look healthy.

Take care of yourself. Make a goal of looking and feeling your best. Remember that the whole point of this auditioning process is to have the client see you and want to hire you to represent his product. A person with a good, healthy, positive feeling about himself is very attractive to casting directors and clients.

DEALING WITH REJECTION

This can be a tough one! Sometimes it seems the most vulnerable people in the world end up in this business in which there is probably more personal rejection than in any other business I can think of. Of course, there are also great personal triumphs, but they're hard to remember when you've just been turned down for the fifth time in a row and you can't even remember the last time you had a victory.

Your point of view is going to determine whether or not you will make it in this business. That's not a simplification; it's a fact. As in all aspects of life, what happens doesn't matter nearly as much as how you react to it.

Let's put things into perspective. First of all, when you are rejected by a casting director or client, they are not saying that they don't like *you!* What they're saying is that they don't think you are right for this project. Either they are right because they are thinking of this character as a different type of person than they think you are, or they are not aware enough of you to know that you could be perfect in the role, or they are making this decision for any of about four thousand other reasons, most of which actually have little to do with you.

In this business, you are always going to lose more than you win. That is a given. Get used to that fact right now, then let it go. You might look just like the client's ex-wife whom he detests. The client's daughter could have just eloped with someone who looks like you. You could have done the best audition in the world and you wouldn't have gotten the part.

There are millions of reasons why it might not have worked out. If you emotionally beat yourself up every time you don't get a part, you're destined for the loony bin. You will be very unhappy, and your work will suffer for it.

Professional actors don't neurotically crumble every time we don't get something because we know that, as stated, we're always going to lose more than we're going to get.

It goes with the territory. It's part of the job. If we don't get a particular role, we take a moment to ask ourselves, why not? What did I do (if anything) that I shouldn't have done? Was there anything that I should have done? How could I have handled this better? Is there anything at all to be learned from this?

If anything could have been done differently, identify it. If it's something tangible that you can work on right away (like not handling the dialogue very well), get to work on it. If it's intangible (like an attitude or a certain approach), file it away. Incorporate it in your next audition. You'll be all the better for it. If you can't pull a lesson from it, then let it go. Sometimes you can't.

That's another thing we have to live with in this business: the fact that there are many things that are just not in our control. We try to influence them as best we can, but even Babe Ruth didn't hit a home run every time. Neither will we.

Handling rejection in a healthy manner may be one of the hardest things to do, but it is also one of the most necessary.

STAYING POSITIVE

Sometimes life can get hard. Staying positive is easy when things are going well, but it's a little harder after you've just lost your third part to that other actor that you don't even think is all that good, plus your rent is two weeks overdue and your car is starting to ping.

May I take this moment to ask you to reconsider before you spend too much time complaining about it? (Deal with it, yes. Grumble about it, no.) There are people in this business (like many other businesses) who tend to be negative. Gripe sessions are very common to some. Actors get together with other disgruntled actors and trash the industry, trash the casting directors, defile reputations, and come up with very creative reasons as to why so-and-so keeps getting parts instead of them, etc.

Complaining, like most emotions, is habit forming. I'm sure you know at least one person who always responds with a negative comment, no matter what you say. ("Boy, it's a pretty day today, isn't it?" "Sure, considering that we're all going to die sometime.")

Being negative makes it practically impossible to enjoy your life, let alone enjoy your career. I have a real aversion to negative people and have had to let a few friends go over the years just because of that. I don't want to be brought down all the time. People can sense negativity more than you may know.

When I first arrived in Los Angeles, a young, green, twenty-two-year-old from Wyoming, I'm afraid I was susceptible to anything. I didn't have a clue as to what was going on out here. My first agent, Dick Clayton (one of the great gentlemen in the business) realized this and, anticipating any future problems, warned me to stay away from a certain bar. It was a show-biz-type hangout bar, and of course I wondered why he wanted me to avoid going there.

He explained that it was a hangout for out-of-work actors who sat around and griped. He didn't want me exposed to that kind of negativity. Being a curious sort, I had hardly left his office when I decided to go there and see what he was talking about.

Well, I was there about fifteen minutes and never returned. He was absolutely right. Negativity permeated the place. If misery loved company, I think she had her own barstool in that place. Maybe these actors who weren't making it found solace in the company of others who weren't making it either, but being in that environment was certainly not conducive to turning their lives or careers around.

Once you get in the habit of looking at things negatively, it's hard to get out of it.

I don't mean to scare you off show-biz hangouts. Some of them are quite fun. This one just happened to have a bad reputation and lived down to it. We actors are sponges. Be careful of the energy you encounter on a regular basis.

Happiness is a habit, too.

The best way for you to maintain a healthy, positive point of view is to create for yourself a world that you are comfortable living in. Odds are that you won't be starting out that way, but that's all right, too. Things are appreciated more when you've had to work for them. Make creating a healthy, secure personal lifestyle a goal, a main priority. It will reflect in your work and serve you well.

I have had the good fortune of living happily and well in this business for nearly forty years. It can be done, and not just by megastars, but sometimes you do have to work at it.

WORKING WITH CASTING DIRECTORS

There are a lot of emotions flying around the audition process. Show business attracts a wide range of personalities, not all of whom are compatible all the time. You are not going to love every casting director you meet, nor will all of them love you. Don't worry about it. Being loved by everyone is not necessary.

Trying desperately to make everyone love you is wasting your time and dissipating what you should really be doing: making them respect you. Create a good, solid, professional understanding and relationship with these people, have them recognize and appreciate your talent and ability. Professional respect—*that* is the relationship to pursue.

It's important to realize that casting directors see and deal with a lot of people on a daily basis. Developing a good relationship with them does not mean being "the personality kid" or hanging around after or during the audition trying to talk to them. Even asking about their family—forget it during an audition.

People who try to chat up casting directors during interviews take way too much time (which is inconsiderate and nonprofessional) and end up boring them, which is not conducive to their asking you back.

Some casting directors are not noted for their people skills, and some have bad days now and then, just like you or me. Don't worry about their attitude. Stick to the professional guidelines we've been talking about and you'll do fine.

You see, they need you. They want you to succeed very much. They want you to be wonderful. They want you to solve all their problems.

The casting director's job is to find the perfect cast for each particular job. They are assembling people to show to the clients, who will have the final say on who is chosen. If the clients don't like the people this casting director brings to them, they'll find another casting director.

The casting director wants you to be so good that the clients will love you. You want her to feel that you're the actor who can do just that. That kind of trust and acknowledgment is gold in this business.

The best way to start and maintain a good relationship with a casting director is to always be reliable and never cause problems. Find out what they are looking for, be it, do it, get out of there, then forget about it. Seriously. Don't spend days fretting about whether or not you're going to get something. If they want you, they know how to get in touch with you.

You'll see the same casting directors many times. As you get to know them, conversations may start up, or not. If it happens, it happens. Don't force the issue. Over the years I've dealt with a great many casting directors, and most are, and always will be, on a "Hi, how are you? Let's get to work" basis. Even with the ones who have become friends, the friendship waits until after business hours or at least to a time when no auditions are taking place.

Consideration of their time is very important. They'll appreciate your awareness.

WORKING WITH CLIENTS

The care and handling of clients is a little different from working with casting directors. By *clients,* I mean the representatives not only from the maker of the product itself, but also the ad agency people who came up with the commercial you're auditioning for. Sometimes the copywriter is also in the room during the audition, as is the director for the spot. You will meet these people at the callback.

Chapter 10 is devoted strictly to the callback, so there's no sense in going into it now, except as relates to our topic, attitude.

If you are going to get the job, these are the people who are going to give it to you. The casting director's job was to get you here—that's all. The final decision rests with these people.

Some clients have had experience with actors and film and are quite savvy, while others have no idea what is going on. They come in all shapes and sizes: young, old, nice, irritating, bright, and not so bright. Regardless, dust off your company manners. You are there not to judge but to be judged.

Often clients don't know exactly what they are looking for but feel they will know it when they see it. When you walk into the audition room, tell yourself that *you* are what they have been looking for. You are going to solve their problems. They need look no further for the casting of this role, and you'll show them why.

Your job is to set the client's minds at ease. You do this by being nice (not gushy), solid, knowledgeable. Show them that they can trust you, that their commercial is in good hands with you.

Realize also that they are people. Although anyone can have a bad day, some clients I've dealt with have been downright rude. I try to never let it bother me because I know they have very tough jobs. We have no idea what's going on with them. Many times actually keeping their jobs depends on getting just the right person for this account. (How would you like that kind of pressure?) Sometimes they are hiring people for spots in which the actor they hire will make more money than they do. That can be hard on the ego.

Make it easy for them. Be the soft-spoken savior. You're looking for work. They have jobs. If you do a good job, you just may help them keep theirs. They like that.

In dealing with everyone, remember "courtesy is not a sign of weakness."

KEEPING IT SIMPLE

A friend of mine met Walter Matthau a number of years ago and was thrilled. He was a great Matthau fan and proceeded to gush unmercifully over the poor man. He took scenes apart, asking him how he did such and such a move, or how he came up with certain reactions, and on and on.

Matthau calmly let my friend continue to prattle on until he was finished. He then said, simply, "I just pretend."

As we all know, there's a bit more to it than that, but keeping it simple in your own mind is a fine attribute. This simple clarity is also a good attribute to carry over to your acting and your auditioning (perhaps even your life).

5

Competition

SOME PEOPLE HAVE TROUBLE WITH COMPETITION. THEY VIEW it as something nice people just don't do. If you happen to feel like that, here's your chance to reevaluate, because as a professional actor, you're not only going to need to compete, you'll have to become good at it. Second only to athletics, show business involves more active, ongoing competition than any other business I know.

Every job you get throughout your career will be yours because you won the competition for the role. Sometimes you will be cast simply because the way you look is perfect for the role. Sometimes the client will instantly fall in love with you. Sometimes you may get it because you outperformed the other actors. Or the reasons could be some combination of the above. (Of course, if you don't get the role, these statements still apply for the other guy.)

Later, when you have years of experience behind you, occasionally someone you've worked with before will just openly hire you for a job. Incidents like these, unfortunately, don't happen often enough to live on. You're going to have to face it: to function as a professional actor, you will have to learn to compete and win.

HEALTHY VERSUS UNHEALTHY COMPETITION

What we're going to do in this chapter is narrow the competitive odds as much as we can in your favor. This chapter works closely with the previous one on Professional Attitude. Much of how you approach the competition aspect of auditioning is also attitudinal.

There are many different types of competition. Let's look at them a minute. As mentioned, in the minds of many people competition has a negative connotation. When they try to picture competitive people, they don't like them very much. They certainly don't want to become one of them.

People like that have a distorted view of healthy competition, and that's what we're talking about here: *healthy* competition.

What I'm talking about is a gentle, steady, effective level of competition that will serve you well the rest of your life. You've got to live with yourself. You've got to like yourself—a lot! You have to respect yourself and feel honestly that you deserve whatever it is that you are going after. Whether it's a job, a sports match, or a relationship, how you think of yourself may tip the scales as to whether you achieve your goal or not.

First of all, keep *hate* out of it. You don't have to hate the other actors to compete effectively with them; in fact, this emotion would get in your way considerably. (You know how hate shows. You can see it and sense it. Do you want to walk into an audition room emanating a feeling like that? I don't think so.)

The best way to view your fellow actors is to respect them. You're going to pit your best against their best, and they are good. You're going to have to be just as good or better to win this. If you belittle or underestimate your competition, you will most likely underestimate the quality of performance you have to bring to the game to win. You don't want to do that.

Rather than a war, this is really more "Survival of the Fittest."

SELF-MOTIVATION

I'm going to make what may seem to be an obvious point, but you would be surprised how many otherwise bright people don't seem to grasp this principle. To put it simply, if something doesn't work, try something else.

Some people get an idea of what they think acting is all about or how they think an actor should act, and they have little or no success at all! But instead of reevaluating their approach, they work harder at what didn't work in the first place.

If your pictures are not getting any response, sending out twice as many of the same shots probably isn't going to help much. If you've tried really hard to make friends with the casting directors but haven't been successful, trying even harder to become friends with them is probably not the approach you should take.

If something doesn't work, try something else. And if *that* doesn't work, try something different. Come from a whole new direction. Perhaps you should try for a different type of head shot? (Are you sure you nailed your category with the first one?) Perhaps you were trying to appear successful (and thereby professional) but came across cocky and arrogant instead (time to rethink it). Maybe you'd be better off pursuing the casting director's respect rather than his friendship?

You have to be a self-motivator in this business. (Waiting for the phone to ring does not count.) It's all up to you. Other than auditions, there are no set hours, no time clocks, nothing you have to do. You have to decide what you want to do and how you are going to do it, then go out and do it!

A friend of mine told me a story about Jack Nicholson that may or may not be true. The point, however, is a good one.

When Jack was a young actor just starting out, a bunch of his friends were heading out to the beach. It was a nice sunny day, and the surf was perfect. Jack turned them down, saying he would get together with them later that night, after business hours.

The other actors cracked up. Business hours? He's trying to be an actor! That's right, Jack agreed. That was his job. If he wanted to succeed, shouldn't he put as much time into his profession as anybody else did for theirs? He thought he should, so that's what he did.

Is it necessary to remind you that Jack has risen to the absolute top of his profession? Hmmmm.

SELF-IMPROVEMENT

To steal another phrase, "You want to be the best you can be." This is a good goal. Try to get and stay in the best physical shape you can reach, try to be emotionally healthy about yourself, this business, and life in general, and try to be as mentally sharp as possible.

The people you are competing with are not dummies. Going back to our "natural selection" analogy, the weak ones don't last long. There are many facets of this business that require having a good mind and using it. Plus, in the course of a career you are going to be portraying and dealing with all sorts of people in different walks of life, under different types of stresses and different situations.

Broadening your knowledge and expanding your life experiences will only add to your ability to understand better where your character is coming from and help you portray it.

Read books. Ask questions. Listen and learn. You'll be a better person for it. You'll be a better actor. Tommy Lee Jones and Natalie Portman have degrees from Harvard! Jodie Foster graduated from Yale. Kris Kristofferson was a Rhodes Scholar. Who'd have figured?

The best and the brightest have a tendency to rise to the top of whatever profession they attempt. Make yourself one of them. Your self-image will reflect that. Other people will read it as ability, confidence, and strength of character. Not entirely bad qualities to have.

It is also imperative that you feel good about yourself. To be effective, a salesman must believe in his product. You are a salesman when you are auditioning. You are trying to convince the client to buy your services. Your ability to do that will determine how successful or not your career will be.

Another point to keep in mind: you never know when a break may come along. You may be coming off a three-month dry spell when the opportunity of a lifetime comes along (this business is like that). If you had let yourself go during your slump, you would probably not perform at your best during the audition and might be unprepared to take advantage of the opportunity.

Get and keep yourself as close to the top of your game as you can. You've got to be prepared to shine at every audition or you will lose it to someone else who outshines you.

FINAL POINTS ABOUT COMPETITION

To wrap up this chapter, let me mention a couple of other things. First, don't carry this competition thing too far, as with a partner. Commercials often have more than one person in them. Sometimes quite a few. Many times, you will find yourself in the audition room with many people at one time, all trying for different parts in this spot.

This is not the time for a solo. This is not the time to try to outdo the others. Common sense must also prevail in your approach to the audition. In a spot containing many people, what do you suppose they are looking for?

Unless otherwise stated by the copy, they will be looking for actors who can work well with each other, who seem to fit together. People whom you could believe are family, or who have been friends for years, or have worked in the same office together. The key word is *together*.

Don't try to compete with these people. For the few minutes that you are all together in the audition room, these are your new best friends (if that's what the copy requires, of course). It's important and necessary to be able to work with other actors. Dust off your acting lessons. Listen!

Here's a tip that will get you a lot of work. I realize, of course, that no one gets into this business to audition. We got into it to perform. However, as we've seen, we are dealing with considerably more auditions than performances. Since our personal goals not only include being successful in this career but also being happy and feeling fulfilled, how can we do that when we're spending so much time auditioning?

Simple. Treat each audition as a performance. No, don't groan; I'm serious. There are no auditions! Only performances! The client and camera are your audiences. They have asked you there that day to perform for them. You will do this to the best of your professional ability, then thank them graciously and sincerely for allowing you to perform for them and for being your audience (not in those words, of course), and then leave.

This attitude will give you a sharper, more complete approach to the copy, give you a much better demeanor during the audition, ensure that your work will be more solid and better thought out, and make it possible for you to gain performance experience while auditioning. You will also feel much more fulfilled and be happier.

That's a lot of good stuff to receive in exchange for a simple shift of mental focus. Try it. I think you'll be amazed.

Finally, here's a tip for the hard-working professional. What do you do when you have an audition at the end of a day in which you've been working (at anything) and you're tired? You're not in the mood. You're thinking seriously of skipping the audition because you're afraid you wouldn't do a very good job anyway.

By all means, *go!* You will be surprised at how many times this will end up working for you.

One of the biggest problems actors have in audition situations is trying too hard. They're trying to anticipate every possible nuance, trying to fit every skill they've got into this twenty-second scene, while also trying to impress the client with how wonderful they are. It's usually too much.

You're probably the fifty-third actor to try this scene that day. The last thing the client or casting director wants to see is a bunch of fancy dancing. They want to see the scene done realistically and well—period.

When you are tired, that's what you do. You don't have the energy for all of your fancy moves. You go in, cut to the chase, do it, and get out. That happens to be exactly what people want to see when casting.

I'm certainly not suggesting that you act tired. No. You will always need to show some energy in an audition, but not having *too much* energy (not being "wired," in other words) will allow you to come across at a very real level. It can keep you from overdoing it.

So, if the situation arises, don't view it as a negative. It could end up working in your favor.

6

Preparation: The Actor

REMEMBER WHAT WE DISCUSSED EARLIER PERTAINING TO actors viewing their acting careers in two different categories: that of Film & TV and then Commercials? The thought seems to be that even though the basics are similar, different skills are required. Not true.

Acting is acting. The script will be shorter, the character usually won't have quite the depth or as much color as many theatrical roles, but you still have to bring believable life, on film, to a character who may be your type but is not you. That's acting.

The more experience you have, the more confidence you'll have in your abilities. That confidence is gold. Not cockiness, not arrogance, not trying to act confident, but the inner confidence radiated by people who feel they have a genuine ability to do what they're doing. You want those feelings emanating from you. You need to feel good about your work.

If you don't feel that way about yourself and your ability now, then that's your next job. Next to physical, mental, and emotional health, confidence in your ability is the foundation of a successful acting career (and not just in commercials).

Let's see if we can come up with a few things that may help boost your confidence.

READING

To be a good actor, it helps greatly if you are a good reader. When you first audition with your script, you have had only a few minutes to analyze it. You certainly won't have time to memorize it (unless it's just a line or two). Usually you'll find yourself still reading most of the copy in the audition. Even so, you do not want to sound like you are reading.

This may not seem like a talent to you, but you would be surprised to discover how many people can't do it. You should hear most copywriters read their own copy. They're terrible! And they wrote it!

An actor is definitely needed to portray the writer's ideas on film, but in order to do that, you've got to be able to read the copy with enough ease and conviction to get the part in the first place.

If you are not a good reader, work at it. Stilted or unnatural delivery will hold you back considerably. A good way to practice is to read a newspaper out loud. Then do it standing, facing your TV, using it as the camera. When you get more comfortable reading, try looking up and returning back to the page.

Track your finger down the side of the paper while you are reading. Looking away isn't going to help much if you lose your place. Try to speak as naturally as you can. Just talk, as if to a friend, perhaps to your best friend.

A good way to practice reading for commercials is to read print ads in a magazine. They are usually short, have a setup, a payoff, and a *point*. We'll get into that more in the next chapter when we concentrate on the copy, but now, we're concentrating on you. The more comfortable you can be with reading aloud, the better your auditioning will be.

NATURALNESS

Commercials are really just little scripts, little stories that have to be told believably. Your job as an actor may be to convince the audience that Carlson's BBQ Sauce is the absolute best you've ever tried and you've been able to think of little else since you first tried it! As silly as it may seem to you, the audience still has to believe you. (If you like it so much, maybe they will too.)

If your performance is unnatural, the audience won't give the product a second thought. If you're auditioning, the client won't give you a second thought. Even though you are an actor, you never want to be caught acting. Whether you have memorized your lines or are reading, your delivery should be no different from the way you would sound if you were talking.

A good way to check this is to talk to someone normally, then pick up something and read it to them, or quote some lines that you have memorized. There should be no difference between your natural speaking voice and your performing voice (unless it's a different character. If it is, read something closer to you.).

You can even do this yourself. See if you slip into *actor mode* when you start performing. If so, you've got something else to work on. Practice talking, then reading, and have the two seamlessly flow.

This is not really that difficult to do if you're a decent reader, but you need to be aware of the concept. Practice it until you get the feeling of it. Once you recognize the two feelings, slipping into actor mode as opposed to reading and performing naturally, you won't even have to think about it. You'll just go for the natural feeling.

The direction you will receive more than any other is to "have fun with it." If it's a lighthearted commercial, prepare for it that way. The prevailing wisdom is that the more the audience likes you, the more apt they will be to listen to you. The more you can keep it light, the more fun you can have with it, the more appealing and effective you will be.

For audition purposes, the above is even truer. Your purpose in auditioning is to convince the casting director and client that you are the one to do their commercial. The more they like you and identify with you, the closer you'll be to booking the spot. (Remember that I'm not talking about friendship here. I'm talking about them liking your performance and believing your relationship to the product. That's what's going to get you the job.)

Any preparation you do as an actor or with the script must not show. We learn how to act in order to act without having it look like we have learned how to act. Every time you perform the script, whether auditioning or performing, it should sound like an improvisation. You are thinking up the words you are saying about this product and you're doing it for the very first time.

Another little trick that makes everything sound a bit more like a real person is to stutter. Not actually stutter, but use it as a technique to make it sound like you are really thinking about what to say next: i.e., "I-I-I didn't know what to do next." "Do you really think that...that he'd do that?" (Don't make every thought sound memorized.)

REHEARSAL

Many commercials contain two or more people. When you are involved with that type of spot, try to rehearse with another person. If you know whom you're going to be reading with, get together with them. Go out in the hall if you feel it may bother other actors in the room. Even if it's not the person you will eventually read with, rehearsing with another actor always helps.

Remember what we said about commercials still being acting, especially scene commercials. The same rules apply here as in doing any other scene. The basis of all acting is listening and reacting accordingly. That is no less true here.

Whatever your partner is saying, it's the very first time you've ever heard her say that. You don't know what she's going to say until she says it. Rehearse with that thought in mind. Everything is being done for the first time.

Don't rush through your rehearsal. Whether you are with a partner or not, read the copy in real time. If you don't want to go out in the hall and say it aloud, read it to yourself but move your lips. By doing that, you will be reading it at the speed with which you talk, not the speed at which you read (which usually are two very different speeds).

One thing that has lost a lot of jobs for actors is socializing in the waiting room. As I mentioned earlier, the actors you compete with will, over time, become friends. You'll find you have more and more in common as time goes on, and many actors just love to talk.

However, keep in mind that this is your rehearsal time! Waiting room time is usually between ten and thirty minutes, sometimes less. That's all the time you have to read the script, study the story board (which shows you what the video portion of the spot will look like), find and get comfortable with an approach and do it enough times in your head (or aloud) that you are comfortable with what you are going to do, plus you should memorize at least the first and last lines.

If you get caught up in kibitzing with your fellow actors, you're wasting valuable time. Wait until you both have read, then meet for coffee or chat by your cars outside. Don't waste audition or rehearsal time getting caught up on the latest gossip.

If another actor is doing this to you, just tell them that you want to take a little more time with the script and how about if you meet him outside in a few minutes? I promise you, no actor is going to take offense at that. In fact, if you book the spot and the other actor doesn't, he will remember this exchange. He won't be quite so ready to visit next time.

GENERAL OBSERVATIONS

You should feel comfortable with the audition you are about to give and feel ready to perform. Put on your company manners (easy, natural, yet capable) and enunciate. Let the clients know you can intelligently get their message across.

At least the first and last lines of the copy should be memorized so that you can deliver them looking straight into the camera (if it's a spokesperson read), or fully on your scene partner (if it's a partner read). The more other lines you can have down, the better. Being able to look away from the cue cards or script during the audition enables you to be much freer than if you were glued to the copy. The more you can do this, the more natural your reading will sound.

Remember that most commercials deal with BIG emotions. You *really* have a bad headache. You *really* love my famous Carlson's BBQ Sauce, and you are openly *excited* about how well your car runs since you changed to a better brand of motor oil.

Never be afraid of being too big. Every director knows it's much easier toning an actor down than bringing one up.

TASTING

You may get a surprise the first time you audition for a commercial involving tasting. Nine times out of ten, clients will want you to react instantaneously to the product's wonderful taste the millisecond it hits your mouth. "That's not realistic," you might say. "I wouldn't even have time to taste it."

True, but that's the way they want it anyway. Time is so short in commercials that they don't want to waste a second (literally) while you decide if you like it or not. They will usually want you to love it instantly, so be ready.

This is another one you can learn from TV. Watch how the actors handle it in the spots already running. Yes, it's unnatural, but your job is to make it seem as natural as possible.

If you do get a chance to actually taste something, have your thoughts go inside. Try to feel the shape of what you've eaten or really concentrate and try to feel what color it is.

A person's face changes when they go inside. It doesn't matter what you are actually doing, what shows is that you are giving this tasting process serious attention, and the client's product requires no less. When you finally smile at the wonderful taste, the audience will feel that it wasn't a rash decision. It works, but be prepared for the quick taste first. That's what they usually go with.

A final tip for special circumstances that sometimes occur: don't be afraid to mimic or imitate other actors or accents that you've heard, especially if you're not that great an impressionist. If you are, forget it. My point is this: if you're a great impressionist, then all you would be doing is acting like some other actor. Not something you really want to do.

However, if you're not that great at imitating people, you may try to duplicate them but be so far off that you've actually created something all your own. Give it a try and see what happens.

A few years ago I was doing an introduction film for a line of robots that hadn't come out yet. My film was to introduce them to the store buyers. There was lots of smoke, bubbling pools, and mood. I was supposed to be walking through the middle of all this talking about how great these robots were. It wasn't working.

I could tell that the clients weren't pleased, and it didn't seem right to me either, so I started experimenting. One approach that I came up with was a very clipped, Rod Serling type of read (à la Twilight Zone). They loved it. It fit into the mood perfectly.

I was a bit surprised when I heard the commercial. I suppose you could tell what I was trying to do, but I missed Serling far enough to create a highly dramatic voice style of my own (which I've used in other commercials since). If I had done a dead-on Serling imitation, they probably wouldn't have gone for it.

Well, not only did the film go well, but they asked me to do the voice for all their commercials, which I did. The fact that I haven't retired yet is testimony that in spite of their spots, which were actually quite good, the robots weren't. Very disappointing robots, but a good lesson learned by me (and now you). Go for it. Don't be afraid to experiment and try outlandish things in the preparation stage.

You might be very pleased with what you come up with, and so might they.

7

Preparation: The Copy

WHEN AUDITIONING FOR A PLAY, THE ACTOR GENERALLY GETS the script or at least the audition scenes a few days ahead of time. Before the play is performed, he has weeks, sometimes even months to create his character.

When auditioning for movies or TV, the actor usually gets the sides (the audition scenes) the day before or at least can go to the casting office and get the scenes a couple of hours before the actual reading. When shooting the show, he generally has a few days to build his character before filming actually begins.

When auditioning for commercials, the actor gets the copy when he shows up for the audition. Waiting time is usually between ten and thirty minutes. This is the total amount of time the actor has to figure out what the spot is all about and how he is going to perform it. The spot is usually (but not always) filmed within a week of the callbacks, which can follow the first audition as soon as later the same day. Most of the time, though, callbacks follow a day or two later.

The point of the above comparison is to underline the importance of getting as much information regarding this audition as you can as soon as you possibly can. Everything has to be done very quickly. We'll be dealing with how to analyze the copy and prepare for your audition thoroughly and professionally in a short period of time.

GATHER INFORMATION

The information-gathering process starts when you get your initial appointment. Whether you are notified by your agent or the casting director, make sure you learn as much as you can from the initial call.

Where is the audition? What time? What is the product? What is the character? Age range (for certain types)? Spokesman? What is the dress? Do they know what kind of person they want? (For example, a lawyer could be slick, sleazy, intelligent, knowledgeable, kindly, etc. Needless to say, the way you would play each would be very different. Find out if you can.) As good as the directions you get over the phone may be, you won't really know for certain what you're going to be doing until you get to the audition and see the script for yourself.

Agents mean well, but sometimes they don't get all the information. I remember a time I was sent out to be a captain. That was the only information they had. I took a guess and went dressed as if I were auditioning as a police captain. It turned out to be an airline captain. Had I known, I would have dressed differently.

The same with the time I was asked to be a guru. I was anticipating a holy-type person but ended up playing a Charles Manson-like guru. Another illustration of the necessity of staying flexible.

When you first get the copy, check to make sure that the instructions you got from your agent fit the copy you are looking at. If you are prepared to be a businessman in a suit and the copy is about two friends fishing, you've got some questions to ask.

(Incidentally, if somebody just totally blew it [which does happen occasionally], and you are set up all wrong, like in the above example, just take off your coat and tie, roll up your sleeves, and think *fisherman*. What have you got to lose? Actually, you'll look so different from anyone else there that if you do a good job, they'll be sure to remember you. ["Oh, yeah. The guy in the dress shirt."] Always try to make the situation work *for* you. Once again, what happens is never as important as how you react to it.)

Okay, it's time to deal with the script itself. You don't have much time, so you've got to act fast but effectively.

An excellent voice-over teacher and director, Maurice Tobias, suggests reading the last line of the copy first when you don't have much time. The reason for that is to get the point of the spot even in the first reading. Right from the beginning, you know where the spot is going to go.

Also, see yourself in the role right from the beginning. (This is you baking bread. This is you taking your kids to school. This is you with indigestion.) Your commercial character is probably not going to go much deeper than *this is you,* dealing with whatever the commercial deals with. By envisioning yourself in the spot as you first read it, you've already started creating your character for this spot.

Since you have so little time to spend with this copy, you must make your performance choices quickly. As you are getting used to the dialogue, you may want to try it a few different ways just to keep from getting locked into a particular read. Getting too rigid in the waiting room makes it doubly difficult for you if the director tells you a whole different concept once you are in the audition room.

FIND THE POINT

After you know what your general character is in the spot, you must find the point. What are they trying to say with this spot? Sometimes it's not quite as easy as it may seem. You want to look for clues.

Try thinking like the writer. Remember that every word has been painstakingly gone over by the client, then by their legal department to assure it contains nothing that could evoke lawsuits. Every word has been carefully chosen. Why did the writer choose this approach to selling this product?

There is a setup and a payoff in practically every commercial.

The couple has been looking for a new car for weeks. They have many unique demands, kids, elderly parents, etc. Is there a vehicle made that will accommodate everything they need? Yes! The new Ford Explorer!

The new boss is really tough. Your co-workers feel she doesn't like any of them. Then it occurs to you that maybe she just doesn't know how to break the ice with people. She may think *they* don't like *her.* So you order her flowers from FTD from all of you. The smile as she walks out of the office tells it all.

Once you understand the setup and payoff, you start building your performance accordingly. Make it as exciting and interesting as possible. Look to see if there is anything special in the copy that should be incorporated in your reading.

The tone of the spot must also be understood since it will be reflected in your reading. What is the background mood of the copy? Is it happy, sad, fun, silly, informative, sharing, kidding, teaching, trusting? Each word represents a different approach to the copy. The tone is an important part of the point and is a major contributor to how you perform this script.

Watch for recurring words. They are not there by accident. They usually help build toward the payoff, but make sure. Why did the writer choose to repeat those particular words? ("The *new* Chevrolet, with its *new* styling is now available in a whole *new* finance plan." Repeated words like these, will usually build in pitch and intensity.)

Adjectives are also carefully chosen and sometimes need to be romanced. These are the words that paint pictures and make what you are selling vivid, exciting, and desirable. When you are talking about a "thick, juicy, succulent steak," we should hear your mouth water just by saying the words. Look for descriptive adjectives like those and *milk* them.

These words are designed to be professionally caressed. When you say, "Yes, it is a Lexus, and it's mine," let's hear pride of ownership that you couldn't begin to contain. Remember, we're dealing with big emotions here. (The play was the *absolute best* you've ever seen in your life. Your floors have *never* sparkled like that! You are *really* glad you used Dial!)

Find the point of the commercial and make sure you make the point in your audition. The point will also determine and show your relationship to any other actors in the spot as well as (and much more importantly) your relationship to the product.

The product will always be involved in the payoff. It will solve your problems. It is the hero. Life would just not be quite as wonderful without Carlson's BBQ Sauce.

TAKE A PROFESSIONAL APPROACH

As the last line above shows, it's very easy to make fun of commercials, primarily because they take relatively unimportant things and make them extremely important. Do you really point out to your guests how you are not getting water spots on your crystal anymore? Do you drive down the street with a look of smug satisfaction and security on your face because you just got a lube job?

For your sake, I certainly hope not, but you may be doing something like that in a commercial. If it happens, go for it. The absurd examples that I just mentioned would happen to be the point of those commercials. (Your glasses will be so clean that you *could* actually brag about them to company. This particular lube job is so good, it *could* actually evoke feelings like those shown.)

Be very careful about making fun of any copy at commercial inter-views, for a couple of reasons. The first is that you never know who may walk in behind you. You may find yourself out of the running before you begin. ("Oh, you mean that was the *client?*")

Another more subtle reason is psychological. Remember that every-thing we're talking about in this whole chapter is going to take place in a few short minutes. I'm sure you are a wonderfully talented actor, but why make it more difficult for yourself? It is going to be harder for you if you need to make a transition, in a few minutes, from making fun of the copy to trying to sell your ability to realistically, meaningfully perform it.

If you want to joke about the copy afterward when you are far from the casting office, fine. (We don't have to be *too* serious about all this, and some of the concepts are pretty silly.) Just don't do it before your au-dition. Look for the point, rehearse making that point, and believe in it. Everything happens very quickly. You need to have your head into it to deal with it effectively.

Remember to stay loose. In a couple of minutes you're going to enter the audition room and be given the final, actual direction for the spot. If it doesn't track with what you had planned, you will have to change im-mediately.

Put yourself in the role from the beginning and keep yourself there until after your audition. Think your performance out in the waiting room. See yourself in the role as you walk into the audition. Everything else will fall into place naturally.

And, as a sign in one of LA's top voice-casting agencies says, "Don't give your best performance in the car on the way home."

8

The Actual Audition

LET'S GO THROUGH THE VARIOUS STEPS OF AN ACTUAL audition. The example I'll be giving, by the way, is a general major market example. Each audition will be slightly different. In smaller markets they may be considerably different.

In any case, the main points will be the same. Regardless of exactly how it's done, the casting director and the clients are looking for an actor and you're looking for a job. The audition is where you *show* them that you are the person they seek. No matter what else happens, it all comes back to simply that.

First we'll go over the steps of the audition, and then we'll take a closer look.

THE SEQUENCE

1. The interview starts with your agent calling to tell you about the audition and to give you your time, the product, what your character is, and whether or not it's a spokesperson spot.
2. You arrive at the designated place a little early, dressed for this particular part. You also have with you a head shot with your résumé stapled to the back of it.
3. The first thing you do after entering the waiting room is sign in.
4. Now is the time to look at the copy. The first thing you check for is whether the information your agent told you was correct.

5. It's rehearsal time. Work on your reading, and find the point. Work with a rehearsal partner if necessary.

6. It's your turn to do it for real. You leave the copy you've been working on in the waiting area and enter the audition room.

7. The person running the session will ask you to stand on the mark they will have on the floor and will give you directions as to what type of delivery and *feel* they want. Read over the cue cards, aloud if possible. When the camera rolls you will be asked to *slate*, which means they want you to state your name and (if asked) your agent or other information.

8. You then read the copy, perform the spot, and dazzle them. Remember: "No auditions, only performances."

Just like that. Okay, those are the broad strokes. Now let's see what's *really* going on. We want as few surprises as possible, and if there's anything along the way that can actually help us land this spot, we want to know that, too. Right?

Figure 8-1 When you enter the audition room, you may find yourself facing something like this. (Photo courtesy of Jeff Gerrard Casting.)

THE SEQUENCE, IN DEPTH

1. When you are first told about the audition, it's not necessary to ask about the dress if it's obvious. Most of the categories are self-explanatory: businessperson (suit), camper (jeans, hiking boots, flannel shirt, etc.), tennis player, skier, formal, casual, etc.

Most of these are very general and are no problem. Unique situations are the ones you need help on. For example, the character may be described as a doctor off duty. (What's he doing while off duty? Is he working in the yard? Taking his family out to dinner? Is he a buttoned-up, formal kind of guy? You'll need more information on this one.)

Or how about a thirty-year-old daughter taking her sixty-year-old mother out to dinner? (First question is, how formal? Are they going to a really nice place or a comfortable neighborhood café? Is it Mother's Day? Easter? Mom's birthday? This is another one where you could ask a few questions.)

If you're told that it's a spokesperson spot, know that it will probably be just you alone, delivering lines into the camera. It's a good idea to go early on all calls but especially ones like these, because you want to be as comfortable with the copy as possible and sometimes a spokesperson will have a lot to say.

What happens if there's no one waiting when you get there and they can take you right away? You don't want to go right away! Tell them that. Let them know that you just got there and would like a little more time with the dialogue. They will understand and tell you to take your time. Everyone wants you to do a good job.

If you want to spend more time with the copy, you can also let someone behind you on the sign-in sheet go ahead of you if they are ready. If you're being invited in a little early, you could also tell them that you're not totally ready but if you could run it a couple of times with the cue cards in the room you could come in then. Usually they'll say, "Sure, come ahead." If, for some reason, they can't or don't want to, they'll tell you that, too, but it's not going to hurt to ask. (Just don't try it if there are a lot of other actors waiting or if the session is pretty busy.)

2. No matter what picture the agency submitted, this is where you can dust off those head shots that you didn't give your agent (like the cowboy shot, or the one of you fishing). If you have one that's right for this part, bring it.

3. For Union jobs, there will be a SAG or AFTRA sign-in sheet. You sign your name, social security number, the time of your appointment, and the time you arrived. Later, you will fill in the time you leave.

Although most casting directors use these sheets to call the actors into the room in the order in which they came, the real purpose of the sign-in sheet is to protect you from being taken advantage of. If you have to wait for more than an hour, you get paid $36.00 as of 2000.

When you are signing in, you can also see how many people are in front of you. They usually check the actors' names off as they are seen. See how many are not checked in front of you. (Of course, you can get a good idea just by looking around the waiting room, but some may be in the restrooms, outside rehearsing, etc.) This lets you know approximately how much time you've got to get the copy ready to be presented.

The SAG sheet has you mark your age range and ethnicity. These are optional. Since SAG covers extras also, there is a place to check whether or not you will work as an extra.

Most casting directors swear that checking *yes* in the "will work as an extra" box will not color their decision about whether or not to hire you as a principal. Still, there can be a stigma. Many feel that you are either an actor or an extra—you choose.

This is one you're going to have to answer for yourself, knowing the professional climate in your particular market. In some larger markets, actors can work as extras all the time and no one ever knows it. There are different agents, different casting directors and, once on the set, you are working with the first A.D. (assistant director) rather than the actual director, so there is very little cross-over. (Still, actor and extra are generally different occupations.)

In smaller markets, it may be the same person doing everything. In others, it may be wide open. You may be a principal this week and an extra next week. Stating that you will work only as a principal may make you look like a prima donna, or not. The point is that you've got to find out what the attitude is in your market.

There's no right or wrong. Learn what the reality of the situation is for you and handle yourself accordingly.

Incidentally, the difference between a *principal* and an *extra* can sometimes be a narrow one. If you have lines you *will* be a principal, but many spots don't have dialogue at all. You can have no lines and still be a principal. A principal is generally the one the commercial is following or the one that helps drive the point of the spot.

An extra will be paid a flat fee with no further payment. A principal will be paid more and will benefit from residuals and holding fees if it's a union spot. (If not, the principal will still be paid more, but just a one-time fee.)

Next to the sign-in sheet, many times you will also find a size card. No matter how many hundreds of times you may see this casting director, you will probably be asked to fill out a size card every single time you are there. They do not keep them. Filling them out is self-explanatory.

My suggestion is to look over the copy first very quickly before filling out the size card. This gives you a few more minutes to think about what you're going to have to do to start seeing yourself in this part, plus sometimes you might be called in early.

4. Read over the copy as we have discussed. Now is when you *really* look at it. Here's where you decide on your approach to the material and your main read.
5. Next you rehearse it. Resist the temptation to chat up the good-looking guy or girl next to you and get to work on the copy. If it's a two-person spot, however, you may want to ask someone to read with you. (Perhaps you can meet your neighbor after all.)

By looking at the sign-in sheet, many times you can figure out which person you will be reading with. If you can, it would be best to rehearse with that person. In any case, now is the time to quickly get an idea in your mind how you are going to approach this copy. Go out into the hall and do it aloud, if you wish.

As you build your performance, remember that in commercials, as in any acting, what just happened sets the mood and tone of what's happening now. Know what happened the moment before your scene starts. Use that moment to start your scene with some momentum.

This is the time and place to make an impact and an impression immediately.

Around this time, someone working there may ask you for a Polaroid. This will be stapled onto your size card and will be used in conjunction with your head shot when the clients later pore over all the tape and pictures deciding on their choice. Take the Polaroid in the character you are there to portray. (The Polaroid is to show definitely what you look like *now*.)

6. It's "show time." The casting director, or whoever is running this session, will escort you into the audition room. You walk into the room as the character they want.

Sometimes there are two or more people in the room, sometimes just one. It will be made obvious to you who is running the audition. You may cursorily meet the others (or not) and then get to work.

Even if this is just a cameraperson, listen closely. They will still know more about what the client is looking for than you do.

Now is the time to ask the cameraperson how tight the shot is and what are the parameters. He'll tell you beltline or tight-head or starting with a full shot, moving in to head and shoulders, etc. This tells you how much room you have to move without stepping out of the shot.

If you have any other questions, now is the time to ask them. Even if there are other people in the audition room with you (clients, ad agency people, etc.), if you have been receiving your instructions from the cameraperson running the session, direct your questions to that person. If the others in the room want to chime in to clarify something, they will, but don't go over the head of the person running the session. They don't like that. (Besides, this year's cameraperson is next year's casting director.)

Read over the cue cards. Make sure you can read them comfortably. Cue cards are all handwritten, and some people's writing is better than others. Read the cards as quickly as possible. Make sure that the dialogue on the cards is the same as what you've been studying. Sometimes they'll change one little word, and it will throw off the rhythm of the read you've been working on.

Know that they are not going to rewrite the cards for you, so even if you have a little trouble reading them, get as comfortable as you can as quickly as you can. That's what you're going to have to deal with. (I don't mean to scare you. This happens very seldom. Most of the time they are just fine, but occasionally . . . !)

(Later in this chapter, we will deal with how to handle cue cards in an audition situation.)

7. The person running the session will usually allow you to have a rehearsal, trying it aloud with the cards. If not, you can ask for one. If there are more than just a couple lines of dialogue, I would suggest it. Any opportunity to rehearse, real time, in front of the camera, in the actual spot you will be doing it, should be taken advantage of.

Many times you will also be asked for profiles. If so, turn quickly in each direction. (Please resist making clever comments at this time. It basically just shows that you are nervous. Also, since you're probably the fiftieth person the clients are going to be looking at on tape, their sense of humor will have left them a long time ago.)

If pertinent to the spot, they may also ask your height, your age, or your particular experience with something like precision driving, skiing, or scuba diving. (Slate and chat in character.)

Try not to stand looking straight into the camera. This has a tendency to make a person look stiff. Give it just a little angle, and do the same with the Polaroids they may take. When all this has been taken care of, the person running the session will say "action" or give you a go-ahead sign.

> 8. The camera's rolling. Entertain them. Be easy, charming, don't rush, but give them good, positive energy, making sure that you *make the point* of the spot. Make it come alive. *Be* the person they are looking to find. Remember the end of the scene is not when you finish your lines but when the director (or the session runner) says "Cut." Stay in character and keep your energy level up until then. After that, thank everyone in the room and leave. Don't overstay your welcome.

It is not necessary for you to come out into the waiting room and tell the other actors what they'll be doing in there. (Being nice is one thing, shooting yourself in the foot is another.) Nor is it necessary or very professional to hang around the waiting room talking to people. You didn't want anyone bothering you while you were preparing; give your fellow actors the same courtesy.

Technically, you don't have to sign out unless you have been kept waiting for more than an hour, but some casting directors like you to do it anyway.

When you leave, try as much as possible to put the interview out of your mind. The more auditions you go on, the easier this will become.

Sometimes you feel awesome in the waiting room but didn't feel that you did the spot nearly as well in the actual audition. Above all, don't apologize! Don't tell them how much better you can do it than that. You had your chance. Learn from it. The next one will be better.

Besides, you may have come across a lot better than you thought.

Example: A few years ago I auditioned to be the voice of Dial soap. All I had to say was, "Aren't you glad you used Dial? Don't you wish everybody did?"

Now, how difficult can that be? Well, I couldn't satisfy myself with what I was doing. I seemed too stilted, the music of it seemed off, the rhythm. I didn't feel I was making the point correctly. I felt so bad during the actual audition that I came very close to letting the casting director know that I would not feel bad if he didn't include my audition tape with all the other actors vying for the part.

That's how bad I thought I was! I felt I'd embarrassed myself already and I didn't want to embarrass him. Anyway, I decided to keep my mouth shut, figuring that he probably wouldn't send it in anyway.

And, of course, I got it. I was the national spokesman for Dial soap for five years, usually having between four and seven national spots running at one time for them.

Needless to say, I've never even thought about asking to be left off a reel again. What may not seem right to you or me may be just what the client had in mind.

CUE CARDS

Since dealing with cue cards in a spokesperson audition is something you will be confronted with constantly, let's take a closer look at what is involved.

As in the picture on page 61, the cards will be placed off to the side of the camera.

Since the cards will be placed next to the camera, you will be pulled in two directions: to focus on the cards because that's where the dialogue is and you haven't had enough time to memorize it all, or to look into the camera and give good eye contact because you know that's how the end commercial will be.

You want your audition to look as close to the actual commercial as possible, but ping-ponging your eyes back and forth from the cue cards to the camera is not going to do it. It drives the viewers crazy and ends up making you look shifty-eyed or untrustworthy. These are not adjectives that are going to get you jobs.

Keep in mind that the clients realize you don't know the lines. They know you got your first look at the script about ten minutes before you went on camera, and they don't expect you to have it memorized. You want to make that work for you.

Here's how.

The very best scenario, of course, is for you to memorize the dialogue and deliver it all right down the throat, which I would suggest if you have only a line or two.

If the dialogue is longer, memorize the first and last lines of the copy. That should be no problem. This will enable you to start and end the audition looking straight into the camera (hence, looking the client right in the eye). That gives you a strong beginning and a strong ending. The rest of the time, stay on the cards.

If you are dealing with a lot of dialogue, try to memorize one line from the middle also. That will give you more eye contact during the read without having your eyes shift back and forth. (Practice looking at the camera on this line during your run-through in front of the camera. Going to the camera is not going to impress anyone if you lose your place trying to come back to the cards.)

If this is done smoothly, it will show the clients what they want to see, which is how you would look doing the actual spot.

If you are comfortable with the dialogue and feel you can easily move your eyes from the cards to the lens and back again without losing your place, let's take it to another level. I call them look-aways, because that's exactly what you do. Most of the other actors will be glued to the cards. Wouldn't it make you look considerably better if you weren't?

Remember that the clients know you just got your first look at this copy a few minutes ago. If you can show a degree of ease with their dialogue at this stage, they will be considerably impressed.

Keep in mind a few things. First of all, there's nothing that says you have to start the audition looking at the camera (copy permitting, of course). If it fits, try to look away at first and then come around during your first line (which you've memorized) to look into the camera.

Then take advantage of any opportunity in the copy that could trigger you to look away. If you mention the product, look at it. If you refer to your office or the weather, look around quickly to take it in.

Perhaps if you're searching for just the right word, you could look away from the camera as you think, and then it comes to you and your gaze returns to the lens. And you will use your memorized last line to end the spot looking solidly into the camera, a good, strong spokesperson finish.

The more ease and fluidity you can show in your audition, the better will be your overall chances of booking.

9

Direction

BEING ABLE TO TAKE DIRECTION QUICKLY AND ACCURATELY IS a skill every commercial actor needs to have. This is a talent that is learned and will come with experience. However, you can shorten the learning curve considerably by simply knowing what to look for. Nothing helps the learning process as much as awareness and the desire to do something well.

The actor who gets the job will be the one who most closely resembles (physically and in ability) what the client had in mind for this spot. That's what you're going after. Direction comes to you through clues. Some are given to you, some you will have to ask for, and others will be surmised.

The first direction you receive comes when you get the call from your agent. The information may be sketchy, but it forms the basis that you will add to. Other than the audition time and place, you will learn your general character (businessman, mom, camper, etc.). You may have to ask whether or not it's a spokesperson shoot.

Actually, your agent may not know any more than that. If this is a product that you are familiar with, that in itself may give you further hints as to what kind of character they would want—especially if it's a product that is advertised a lot. Look for clues.

If you were called to be a businessman for Advil, you would probably be slightly upscale and well groomed. You would know that because of the type of people they've used in their commercials for years. If you were asked to play a farmer's wife for Advil, you would still probably be the wife of a fairly affluent farmer. *The Grapes of Wrath* and Advil don't seem to go together, do they?

If you are advertising lawn cleanup bags or dog food, your direction from your agent might simply be to look casual. From the subject matter, you would know that something like jeans and a broken-in sports shirt might be right.

If your direction was to be casual but the product was Cadillac or Lexus, your "casual" dress might be slacks and a not quite so broken-in sport shirt.

Basically, it's common sense, but take a moment to assess all the information you have before you go to the audition. By then, you will be stuck with what you are wearing. The rest of the clues will be available to you at the audition.

The first thing you will see at the audition will be the other actors who are up for the same role. It's always interesting to see how they interpreted the call. (Good ideas for future auditions can sometimes be found here.)

By the time you are at the audition, your concentration is on interpretation and delivery of their script. The main source of direction is, of course, the copy itself and the storyboard. They will provide perhaps your biggest clues as to what the clients are after.

Once in the audition room, your session runner will provide more. They will tell you what the client told them. ("They want a nice easy read." or "At first the viewer might think you're a bad guy but then learns you actually work for SOS Alarm and are after the bad guys.")

You may have some questions, but they may not know any more than what they told you. You'll have better luck getting additional information if the casting director herself is running the session. In larger markets, most of the time a cameraperson hired by the casting director is the person who runs the first session. Some are better than others, but all of them know only what the casting director has told them.

Listen to the intent, not just the words themselves, which can sometimes be confusing. The copy and the general directions must make sense to you. You have to understand, at least, what you think they want before you can give it to them. Never be afraid to ask questions.

Sometimes the directions clients leave with the casting director are really tough. The worst example I've run across of how one client actually said they wanted the copy read was "Voice of God, with an edge!" Good luck with that one!

Or how about copy that reads, "Buy now! This sale won't last long. This is your last chance. Buy today! Come on down!" and your direction for the delivery reads, "Easy, conversational, not an announcer, have fun with it."

It'll happen. Surprisingly often you'll get combinations like that—hard-sell copy with soft-sell instructions. Here's where you really have to look at the intent. With the last example, they ask for a conversational read with dialogue that is anything but conversational. The reason they would use directions like that is probably to pull the actor back from a sideshow barker type of read that the copy could easily suggest. Because of the copy, it's got to be an intense type of read, but you could soften it a little by viewing it as if you were talking excitedly to a friend of yours. You feel you have just made the deal of a lifetime and are trying to convince your friend to also take advantage of this stupendous opportunity. They may not believe you, so you have to convince them, and you can do this honestly because you truly believe this is for their own good. They will thank you profusely for turning them on to this deal.

Something like that. If the copy doesn't give you a story that shows you what to do and why, build your own scenario. You'll find that doing this will give you a definite point of view that will keep your read consistent.

(As another example of how out-there directions can sometimes get, an agency producer told a story about something she had done as she was overseeing the music portion of a spot. She had asked the conductor in all sincerity, "Do you think you could have the flutes sound a little more ironic?" Fortunately, she laughed at the absurdity of it, but still, that was what she wanted to know.)

As always, keep flexible. If you get a chance to do something again, ask them what they would like a little more or less of. Then give it to them. Never allow your read to get in a rut. There is practically always a little tweaking that goes on, but by listening and paying attention to the clues, your approach to the copy should be close to what the clients have in mind.

CALLBACKS

In the next chapter we'll look at callbacks in depth, but while we're on the subject of direction, let's see what may be different on a callback.

The two main differences are that you will usually be directed by the actual director who will be doing the spot, plus there will usually be at least one representative from the client or their ad agency.

These are the people who know everything about this spot. One of them may even be the writer. You will usually receive much more information than you had in the first audition. If you have any questions at all about the copy or the type of read they want, now is the time to ask.

Please don't think that asking questions makes you look like you don't know what you are doing. Exactly the opposite! The pros know that they have only a minute or two with these people. It's now or never. Get all the information you need so that you can confidently give them what they are looking for.

Accept all direction gratefully. The director is telling you what you need to do to get this spot. There may be a room full of people behind the camera, but don't get caught up in the activity around you. Focus on what you are there for, and listen!

Warning! You may be extremely handsome or pretty and accustomed to using your looks to help get what you want. Other than looking your best (and looking the part), I would caution you against trying to use your physical wiles on the director (or casting director, for that matter).

This is the quickest possible way to cheapen your image. Besides, in this age of sexual harassment suits, a little flirting during an audition is enough to make the director run the other way.

Even if you are attracted to the director, this is not the time or place for flirtation. If you really want to make an impression, dazzle him with your professionalism. I promise you that it will get you much farther. (Get the job, get to know him on the shoot, and then date him afterward.)

Regardless of who the director is, your attitude toward him should always be one of respect. He is the boss. He is also a major player in deciding who gets this job.

No groveling, however. He is a professional, and you are a professional. Treat him with the dignity and respect his position deserves but do it with the pride and dignity that *your* position deserves. You are two professionals, each needing the other, working together, both winners.

Keep that feeling, keep that pride, keep the mutual respect, and I assure you, you'll have a healthy, productive relationship with the director.

10

The Callback

CONGRATULATIONS! YOU MUST HAVE DONE SOMETHING right. You've made the finals. If you are going to book this spot, the call-back is where you are going to do it. You will now meet the real players. Up till now, you haven't met anyone who could actually hire you for the job. The people you've met could have stopped you if they chose, but they had only the power to say "no."

At the callback you will meet the people with the power to say "yes." This is where you close the deal.

Sometimes there is quite a crowd in a callback room. Running this session, most of the time, will be the actual director for the commercial. She may be the only one you talk to.

Behind her will be from one to twelve (seriously!) representatives from the client and/or the client's ad agency. It doesn't matter to you at all how many people are there. Your job stays the same.

You may not even be introduced to the people behind the director. If you aren't, don't get your feelings hurt. Many people like to totally stay out of the way and let the director work, while others like to be much more involved. You will work with both kinds.

The callback is basically an opportunity for the clients to see first-hand how you and the other actors work. Very few people will actually hire actors from videotape without meeting them in person.

The importance of face-to-face contact with the client during the call-back became clear to me a few years ago when my wife and I went to visit some friends of ours who lived in Texas, about an hour north of Houston.

A week or so before leaving I had gone on an audition for Bose (the speaker manufacturer). I hadn't heard anything from them, so I thought it was safe to get out of town for a few days.

No sooner had we flown to Houston and made the hour-long drive to our friends' house than my agent called, saying I had a callback that afternoon for Bose. The clients were in town and wanted to meet me. Damn.

I reminded him I was in Texas. I hated to miss the callback, but sometimes things happen that way. I suggested he explain the situation to them and recommend they take another look at my original audition tape, and then I went back to my friends.

Fifteen minutes later, he called back. They *really* wanted to see me and would fly me back if I'd come. "When?" I asked. "Now." Good grief.

Not being a fool, I agreed, said "Good-bye" to my wife and friends, drove to Houston, flew to LA (first class, thank you—gotta love SAG!), took a cab to the casting director's office and met the clients.

We chuckled at the situation and discussed the script, which I then did for them a few times. We said good-bye and I took the cab back to LAX, flew to Houston, and drove the hour back to our friends' house and arrived about eight in the evening. My agent had just called to say that I got the part.

A week or so after returning to LA, I flew to Boston for a week of shooting for Bose. Perfect, but I'm sure it wouldn't have worked out that way if they hadn't been able to physically see and meet me. Callbacks are important.

(See? Sometimes this business can be great fun!)

At your callback, if you do meet the clients, be professionally gracious, then get to work. Don't get too comfortable, because you haven't gotten the job yet. This is where you become the very best, most professional person you can be.

The people in that room are preparing to shell out hundreds of thousands of dollars (sometimes more) to film this commercial. They need to be very sure that the actor they hire will be able to perform this spot successfully. Your job is to make them extremely comfortable with you and your ability.

Do not try to schmooze your way into the job. Besides the fact that it would be rather obvious what you were trying to do (these people aren't dummies, you know, or they wouldn't be sitting in those chairs), you would be missing the point. They don't necessarily want someone who *is* nice. They want someone who can *act* nice, and they haven't even decided if they like you yet. Don't push it.

Once again, you have to figure out what they are looking for, but you don't have to start from scratch. You have a really good clue as to what they want: you, and what you did at the audition! If what you did wasn't in the ballpark, you wouldn't be on the callback.

So, if it ain't broke, don't fix it. Dress the same as you did on the first interview, if you feel it was appropriate. If you felt your dress wasn't quite right, now you can correct that.

One big point in favor of wearing the same outfit as the first time is to remember that these people pored over the initial videotape of God knows how many actors and narrowed it down to you and the others in the waiting room. Wearing the same outfit simply makes it easier for them to remember you and what they liked about you.

Remember our discussion about being the character as you walk in the door. This is just as important in callbacks. In the first audition, your focus was to put the best possible audition down on videotape. In the callback, the people are there in person. They are going to be watching you walk in the door, and they'll also have a feeling about you in the first ten seconds. Make that knowledge work for you.

LISTEN

I can't stress enough the importance of listening closely to what the director says to you on the callback. As I mentioned in the last chapter, she's telling you what you need to do to get the job!

Sometimes there are actual discussions between the director and the ad folks as to what they want. If that happens, listen. If you can pick up a tidbit that will help you, fine, but *stay out of the discussion* at all costs! You may have the perfect answer to what they are talking about but, I promise you, they don't want to hear it from you.

You could come up with the best idea in the world, and they may even use it, but you'll never know about it because you will never see them again. Clients and ad people respect actors who are good actors. They do not respect actors who have the audacity to think they could do their job also (even if you could).

Please remember, no matter how anyone acts, they all want you to succeed—they really do—for their own reasons:

THE INITIAL SESSION RUNNER wants you to succeed because it shows that he ran his session well enough for the clients to get enough of a feeling for what you can do to call you back in. He did his job. Yeah!

THE CASTING DIRECTOR wants you to succeed because it's her job to get the client the perfect actor for their commercial. If you get a callback, it shows they like you and consider you a possibility. If you get the job, it is even better. That shows they love you and are pleased with the casting director for bringing you to their attention. (If the clients weren't pleased with anyone, they would have had this [or another] casting director put out another call and a different group of actors would be called in.)

THE DIRECTOR wants you to succeed because he needs an actor he feels he can work with. Although certainly not the final voice, hers is a strong voice as to which actor gets hired. (The client may love someone, but if the director feels the actor won't be able to handle the role or she has a bad feeling about working with him, the client is not going to go over the director's head and hire that actor anyway.) The director is being paid to be there to voice her opinion as to which actor will actually be able to deliver on the set. The director (like everyone else) would like for the decision to be unanimous.

THE CLIENTS AND AD AGENCY PEOPLE want you to succeed because they have an awful lot of money and importance riding on them writing, casting, and filming the perfect commercial for their company. Everybody (even the clients present) has someone to answer to (the CEO is never in the room). They want to be blown away and put at ease. They want to know that by hiring you, this commercial—and maybe even their jobs—will be safe.

(You may think that I am overstating the importance of a little commercial, but remember that for many of these people, making commercials is what they do for a living. That is their only job, and as in so much of show business, they are only as good as their last campaign. It doesn't matter so much what you did as what you can do now.)

So, see? You have a support system in place that you didn't even know about. Everybody really does want you to do well.

TECHNICAL TIPS

You've got the concept by now. Let's look at a couple of other things you should keep in mind if you are to land this job.

Memorize

First of all, try to get off the cue cards as much as possible. This is the second time you have auditioned with this script. You are much more familiar with it now than you were at the first audition. See if you can memorize at least another line or two to deliver into the lens of the camera (if it's spokesperson copy) or can keep your attention more on the product and/or your scene partner (if it's a two- or three-person scene).

Yes, they still know you are auditioning, but these are the finals. Your competition is now all the other actors who also did well enough to get a callback. You've got to bring your performance up a notch or two if you are going to outshine them.

The "Ear"

The "ear" (sometimes referred to as the "bug") has become quite popular in some circles. It consists of a small device that looks like a hearing aid and fits into your ear. It is actually a wireless receiver tuned to the same frequency as a tape recorder/transmitter, about the size of a deck of cards, which you have in your back pocket or purse.

The ear is useful for dealing with large amounts of dialogue. What you do is record the reading you want into the tape recorder. On camera, you then play it back, duplicating out loud what you are hearing in your ear.

It sounds bizarre if you've never tried it, but some people have carved out whole careers for themselves by being very good with this little device. It's owned by the actor and costs about two hundred dollars but costs the production company nothing. They save the expense of a teleprompter and operator.

We'll discuss this topic more in the second half of the book. The reason I mention it here is that more and more actors are starting to use this device on auditions, especially callbacks. I guess they figure it's a good way to impress everyone.

I would suggest *not* using it here, for a very good reason. In a callback, when the powers-that-be are in attendance, many times the client tells the director to give the actor an adjustment in his read—to suggest that he do something he didn't do the first time around.

They will watch closely to see how you (the actor) react to this instruction. Sometimes they do this just to see how well you take direction and how flexible you are (or aren't), which will give them a good idea of what you would be like on the set. They don't want someone who is so stuck on a particular read that they can't get anything else out of them.

The point here is that once you have a certain performance recorded in the ear, you don't have the flexibility to change it at a moment's notice, which is exactly what's required of you many times in callbacks. Nobody wants to take the time now for you to go out, rerecord the spot with the new instructions, and come back and do it again. Time, as always, is money, even in callbacks.

If you've got your own ear and are good at using it, mention it, but sell yourself on your acting ability and your readiness to take direction. In the actual shoot, once the performance everyone wants has been determined, then you can put that into your recorder, but until then, stay flexible and keep your ear in your pocket.

Big Action

Occasionally, you might find yourself involved in what we call "big action" commercials. This includes activities like skiing, swimming, golf, rock climbing, basketball, horseback riding, and so on: a physical skill that you are supposed to have.

As we discussed, some actors will say anything to get a job. Bearing that in mind, few clients are going to book you for their very expensive commercial based on your word alone. If you are supposed to be a good tennis player and you say you are, most of the time the callback will be on the tennis court so you can show them what you can do.

If you have lied, you will look like a fool and will have lost total credibility with the casting director, who will never trust you again. If you are as good as you say, the opposite will happen. Whether you get the job or not, at least you will have maintained your integrity (and that is more important than many people realize.).

I've been to callbacks where seven or eight of us were actually taken up to a mountain so the clients could watch us ski. (Remember the story I told you about the spot I did where they didn't watch us? Actually, I wish they had. I would have been able to compete head to head, and I feel I would have gotten the spot anyway. At least, there would have been no question about my ability. Ah, well, fortunately it ended fine.)

I'm trying to make a couple of points here: never lie (because you will be found out), and don't think you have to be wonderful at everything. You don't. If you've only skied a couple of times but do a mean snowplow, tell them. That may be the type of skier they want.

On the callback where they wanted to see us ski, one of the guys was a professional ski dancer! He was amazing. He could ski backwards, sideways, and could even skate with his skis. One time he came down, literally skiing circles around his partner as she skied down. And he was handsome!

He didn't get the part. I think the clients thought that he was so good no one would identify with him, and they were probably right. The guy who got the job (not me, alas) was a normal guy and an okay skier: exactly what they wanted.

Here's another point to keep in mind. These "big activities," especially if you're good at them, are usually fun. It's very easy to get caught up in the moment and desperately want to beat the other actor at tennis or to make this eight-foot putt, but there's usually more to it than that.

The client generally will not only want someone who can play the game well but someone who really enjoys the game, or is playing with close friends who have been playing together for years (after which they will go and enjoy a cool Coors together), or who loves to ski but couldn't help noticing the cute girl in the blue stretch pants with the lovely Neutrogena complexion, and so on.

There's usually a subtext: something you are thinking or feeling while you are doing this big activity.

I remember a time when a bunch of us were trying out for a beach volleyball beer commercial. We all knew that this could be a big (lucrative) one, so we worked very hard to be the best beach volleyball players in the world. When I didn't hear anything from the agents after a couple of days (I thought we'd been great!), I inquired. None of us had gotten it. We'd all been so intent on playing well that we had forgotten to have FUN, and that's what they were selling, not what good volleyball players we were.

That's how I learned this tip I'm passing on to you: the hard way.

WRAP UP

What will book this spot for you is naturalness (but still with energy), likability, and professional reliability. They need to know you can and will deliver the goods. The callback is your chance to convince the clients that they need look no further than you, because you are the solution to their problem.

You don't do that by being cocky. You do that by being good.

Remember, especially in the callback, that there are no auditions, only performances! Give your best performance for them.

Be a gracious lady or gentleman. Thank them when you leave. Make them want to work with you because of what a pleasure it would be.

Always leave a good impression behind. That's the best way to ensure that the next time you see them will be on the set. That's exactly the way it should be.

TWO

The Art of the Performance

11

The Concept and the Product

THERE IS A CONSIDERABLE DIFFERENCE BETWEEN AUDITIONING for a commercial and shooting it. This part of the book deals with the changes in POV and motivation involved in the actual, final, shooting.

THE CONCEPT

In auditioning, everything you did was targeted toward getting hired. Congratulations! You have done that. Now it's time to perform. Your job now is to make their commercial come to life, to tell the story that the clients feel will sell their product.

Your professional point of view now is twofold. Your first objective is to please the director and clients in your shooting of their commercial. The second is to reach the audience in such a way as to create additional interest in the product. (You may also want to remember that the more successful a commercial is, the more they will use it. The more they use it, the more money you will make from residuals.)

Each commercial is different, with its own point of view and its own point to make. We're back to that again. Except, this time, you're not trying to convince anyone about how good you could be. Now is the time to show them how good you *are*.

You've got to think like the writer again, but you're not in the dark now as much as you were before. The fact that you got this commercial based on your audition readings should tell you that you weren't far off from what they had in mind. Plus, all the cast of characters are there on the set with you, and they are all on your side. They are there to help you.

You've got quite a support team. Any questions you have regarding the script can be answered by the producer, the client, or perhaps even the writer himself. Any questions regarding the performance can and will be answered by the director. There's no competition any longer. You are an integral part of a team now. The collective intent of this team is to present the concept of this spot to the television audience in hopes of heightening awareness and perhaps even creating an open desire for the client's product (which is now *your* product!).

This is when you solidify certain things you were either guessing or surmising during the audition. Now you know (or will soon find out) what the point of the spot is. You know what the writer is trying to say and how he plans to make his point, and you know what you are supposed to do to help bring this about.

In facing the reality that you are, in fact, the one the clients chose to perform their commercial, it's very good to ascertain why they hired you. What did they think you had that the others on the callback didn't have? What are they expecting you to bring to this copy? What are they hoping you will do?

I would suggest asking yourself those questions and taking the time to answer them. If the director and the clients are expecting something from you, it would be helpful if you knew what it was.

It may be nothing more than expecting a nice, easy, comfortable read, or it could be that they feel you have the ability to show that you and your spouse are disagreeing over something but deep down inside, still love each other a lot. They may want you to show that people can still have fun and look great after the age of fifty or that all teenagers are not irresponsible when it comes to driving, or dating, or whatever.

In the same vein another question to ask yourself is "What kind of people are they trying to reach with this ad?"

By knowing the age, sex, and type of the targeted audience, you can create and adjust your delivery accordingly. (Your manner of speaking to a group of eighteen-year-old jocks will be different from what you would use if you were talking to a group of forty-year-old Moms.)

You know what the spot's supposed to do; now you also know what's expected of you to help bring it about.

THE PRODUCT

The product is the star, and you are but a supporting player. Your relationship is like Vanna White to her letters. They are what's important;

she is the mode of delivery. You are the vase, and the product is the bouquet. You get the idea.

If the answers to the following two questions aren't immediately apparent, take a moment and answer them. If the answers still elude you, ask the clients or the ad agency people themselves (remember, you and they are all on the set now and on the same side). Both will love to talk about their product. You'll probably learn more than you ever wanted to know about it, but you certainly will get your questions answered.

It will also make you look good in their eyes because it shows that you care enough about the product to want to really understand it. (Also, notice their intensity and commitment when they talk about it. That might be a good tone to use in your delivery.)

1. What really makes this product different from other products like it?
2. Why is this product really better than any of the others?

Regardless of what the copy says, the answers to those two questions will give you your subtext.

How Does It Make You Feel?

Especially in spokesperson copy, it's good to identify with the audience. View them with compassion and caring. You understand their plight. There was a time when you didn't know how great this product was either, but fortunately those days are gone. Now you know! And you want to share. Why should these good people in the audience not know about this product? It wouldn't be fair to withhold this information. It could be downright cruel.

Anyway, you are there to alleviate any discomfort that may come from not knowing about this superior product. (Now their dishes will be *really* clean, their bankruptcy can be handled quickly and quietly, and their car will smell new forever.)

There's an old advertising adage that says, "You're not selling the steak, you're selling the sizzle." Many times products are sold by how they sound, or look, or how you'll feel after using them.

You don't buy this floor wax simply to have clean floors; you buy it because of the *satisfaction* you'll feel knowing your floors look great. There is *confidence* in knowing that your crystal will not be spotted. There is *pride* in knowing that your kids are getting a good lunch.

When you are representing the product, make sure you know what you are selling. Understand the desired approach. Know what point you are supposed to make about the product and prepare to make that message come through clearly.

Tasting

Remember the two types of tasting we talked about, the instantaneous delight and the slow savor? They'll tell you what they want, but when it comes to actually eating on camera, you might want to bear the following story in mind.

A few years ago I did a KFC commercial. We were supposed to be on the last portion of a roller-coaster ride. We were to come out of this tunnel laughing, having fun, and eating chicken. (I know, I know. I didn't write it!)

Fortunately, I like KFC. I thought this was going to be the easiest commercial I've ever shot. Well, if you pay attention to food commercials, you'll notice that very seldom, if ever, will you see half-eaten food. You usually see nothing but the first bite, and that's the way they want it.

Out of sight in our roller-coaster car were two big buckets. One was filled with chicken, the other was to be filled with what was left of each piece of chicken after we had taken one bite (affectionately called the spit bucket).

I thought I'd go ahead and finish each piece. Why waste food? That lasted about two takes. Soon after that, not only was I depositing the remainder of my chicken pieces in the spit bucket, but I was even spitting out the bite I had taken, and so was everyone else.

Fortunately, the client didn't mind this. They realized that after the thirty-sixth take even the wonderfulness of KFC may wane just a bit. On camera, though, we were loving it just as much.

Since there was so much action in the spot I just described, it's a perfect example of not selling chicken as much as selling the fun and enjoyment you'll have if you eat this chicken.

Beauty Shots

Beauty Shots are close-up shots that show off the product. Sometimes these shots involve the actor. If you happen to be that actor, this is the time to focus your attention on the product. That's what will be asked of you.

The Product is the boss. It's paying the bills, and you have been asked to assist it in its close-up (CU). If it's a steaming cup of Folgers coffee, you will be asked to hold the cup and saucer exactly the way they will set it up for you. You will not jiggle, you will keep it in sharp focus, and if you are supposed to drink you will do so slowly and smoothly, savoring every drop, and return the cup to the saucer, still keeping everything in perfect focus.

If everything does not go as mentioned above—everything!—you will do it again, and again, and again. Twenty, thirty, or more takes are not uncommon for shots like these. As far as the client is concerned, this shot is the most important shot of the commercial. All the flavor, all the goodness that has been set up and paid off in the commercial should show in this shot.

I would suggest using as much time as you can between shots (maybe even while others are taking five) to rehearse your moves. Practice getting the cup to the right level, tipping it just the way they want so the coffee won't flare into the lens, or maybe they want a little light flare. If that's the case, you've got to practice that, too.

Whatever you do, it must be done smoothly and easily. No attention should be drawn to whatever you are doing with the product. It should look completely natural. As you practice your moves, that, above all, is your goal.

Working with the Hero Product

If you've never worked with a *Hero Product* before, the first time may make you laugh inwardly, but keep it to yourself because this is extremely serious business.

If you've been setting up and rehearsing for a close-up product shot of Carlson's BBQ Sauce, you've had a jar that you've been using for rehearsal. Just before cameras roll, however, that jar will be taken from you. You will then be carefully handed THE jar of Carlson's BBQ Sauce.

This is the Hero jar. This jar has flawless glass, a label that is perfect, placed on the jar *exactly* as it should be, and is impeccable in every way. You treat this with the care you would give a baby bird. Usually there are two or three of these heroes but I've done some shoots where there is only one. Needless to say, there is no clowning around with the Hero product.

Props will put it into your hands a millisecond before the shot starts and will take it away from you the instant "cut" is heard.

Treat the Hero like what it is: a perfect representation of a wonderful product, one you are very pleased and honored to be associated with.

12

Rehearsal

PREPARING AT HOME

A good performance begins with good preparation. Your preparation for the shoot begins the moment you find out that you got the job. Your very first action should be to make arrangements to get the copy as soon as possible.

If the shoot is still a few days away from when you are being notified, the final script may not have been finished and approved yet. If not, get on the list to have one sent to you the moment they have a shooting script.

Sometimes they will have to mail it to you. If they can e-mail it or fax it, all the better. Much quicker.

While you are waiting for your script to arrive you can take care of any other related business that needs attention. Do you need a haircut? Color touched up, maybe? Now's the time to take care of it. Is there any wardrobe that you need to supply? If so, make sure you have it and that it's clean.

Are there any skills you need to brush up on quickly? (If you're supposed to be playing basketball in the backyard with your kids but haven't touched a basketball in years, you might want to go to the park and shoot a few hoops just to get a bit more comfortable with it. You'll feel more confident on the set if you're able to deal more with how you are feeling about this moment, rather than having to totally concentrate on hanging onto the ball.)

Should your nails be done? (If you are going to be holding a Product, you might want to consider a manicure. This advice is for both men and women, by the way. The only difference here is that men should have a clear, nonshiny polish.)

Memorization

As soon as you get your script, get to work memorizing it. Read it over a few times, making sure you understand the concept and why each word was chosen.

A good way to get it all to stick is to write it down, then read your own writing out loud, then look away and do it. With short, easy scripts, that might be enough to get it into the memory banks. If so, let it go but return to it many times a day until the day of the shoot. Say it to yourself in your mind before you go to sleep. Do the same thing when you wake up.

If your scene is with another actor or two, use their lines as cues for yours. Don't try to memorize your lines on their own. (When your friend says, "I hear you just got a new car," that is an automatic lead-in for you to say, "Yeah. The new Pontiac. I love it.") Always play the sense of the scene. It makes memorizing much easier.

If what you have to memorize is long and complicated with no obvious cues, you're going to have to work a little harder. You cannot read it out loud too many times. You cannot write it down too many times.

If the words still aren't sticking, break the script into halves or thirds (depending on how long the script is). Take one section at a time, memorizing *the concept* of each. What is it that is being said here? What is the point that's being made? Once the concept has been understood, use the words of the script to get it across.

After the concepts and the points to be made are understood and memorized in the order in which they occur, start memorizing the *phrases* that make these points. Don't memorize individual words. Go from phrase to phrase, then put together the sentences. It makes much better sense that way.

Keep repeating the above until you've got it.

Another thing to look for in the script is how much will actually be shot at one time. If you have two different locations in the spot, you know it will be filmed in at least two different chunks. The same applies if there is a before and after (a setup and a payoff).

Memorize the groups individually. Instead of having one big, difficult script to memorize, you will have two or three much smaller, easier ones.

Your Approach

You can be working on your performance at the same time you are working on memorization. (In fact, please do.) Say the words out loud. Speaking is different from thinking. Experiment with different reads as you do this. Try to anticipate any possible direction you could get, and always rehearse in character.

At this point, there will probably not be any big surprises with the script. They're not going to change the concept of the spot or type of character you are playing from callback to shoot. Most likely, however, a lot of little changes will be made, so get comfortable with your basic read but stay loose enough for a little tweaking.

As you rehearse at home, do it standing or in the position your character will be in during the shoot. If it's not obvious whether you would be standing or not, do it in various positions. The point here is to get and be comfortable, no matter how you end up.

In a spokesperson situation, it's good to give yourself a focus. We discussed earlier how the TV makes a good focal point to practice in front of for auditions. It works for performances, too.

Stand in front of it and pretend that it is the camera. Do your whole scene. Walk into the area in front of the TV, if that's what you are supposed to do. Practice looking away, then coming back to camera, as you do your dialogue. Rehearse your exit, if you have one.

This is an excellent exercise if you haven't done a lot of work straight into the camera lens. It won't seem quite as foreign when you find yourself in front of the real thing.

Also rehearse in wardrobe. Get the feel of doing this copy standing up in a business suit, or lying across your bed in your bathrobe, if that's what you'll be doing. If you don't have the exact wardrobe you will be wearing, get as close as you can.

Your sport coat and tie will give you a similar feeling to the suit they will supply you. Wearing your bathing suit will prepare you for how it will feel to do this copy in their bathing suit.

Your intent is to get as comfortable as possible, at home, with situations that may (or will) occur on the set.

If the scenes you're working on involve two or more people, have someone at home read lines with you. They don't have to be actors. You just need to hear the lines coming at you so you can respond with your lines. These are your cues. This will also help you get the timing and the sense of the scene.

If you can't find anyone to read lines with you, or if you want to re-hearse more than they want to read, a last resort is to read the other person's lines into a tape recorder, leaving enough time in between for you to say your lines. You can then play this tape as much as you want, wherever you want (such as when you're driving), and keep working on your lines.

(This is especially helpful if you have a lot of lines to learn, as in a soap opera. Most commercials are not long or complicated enough to warrant this, but you never know.)

REHEARSING ON THE SET

No matter how much film work you've done or how long you've been in the business, when it's your first day on a new set, the first thing for you to do is get comfortable ASAP. You do that by quickly becoming familiar with your surroundings.

See the set. If possible, walk around in it. Take in as much as you can. Meet the principal players. You will already have met the director and at least one member of the client/ad agency contingency. Greet them and meet other clients you may not have met. Introduce yourself to the script supervisor (See if any changes have been made in the dialogue you've memorized. If so, don't panic. Changes made at this point will be very minimal, and you'll have plenty of time to make the adjustment and learn the new line or two.)

You'll also meet the first assistant director (AD) and, if there are other actors in the spot, introduce yourself to them also. If your character is supposed to be very closely attached to the other actors (i.e., spouse, child, best friends, etc.), make time to get to know them as well and as quickly as you can.

Try to have breakfast together, talk while you both are in makeup. Every little bit helps when it comes to being comfortable with each other.

If circumstances don't allow much "getting to know you" time, just remember that you are not supposed to be in love (for example) with this person you hardly know, your *character* is in love with her *character*. They are very comfortable with each other.

Looking at it in that way may ease the nerves a bit. Still, the more honestly at ease you are with each other, the easier it will be for you to portray those feelings. Always try to do what you can.

The sooner you run lines together, the sooner you are going to know how the real read will go. How you will eventually play this scene is going to depend a lot on what you get from the other actor (just as their performance will be linked to what you give them).

Try to rehearse in the set as soon as possible, whether the cameras are set up or not. Start letting your characters and their relationships come to life in these surroundings. Up till now, your character has only known life in your living room or in your car, but this set is where your character will live. Get your character used to existing in these surroundings.

This set is a part of your character's world. It may be their living room or office. If your character is supposed to be familiar with this room, make yourself familiar with it. It will be easier to convey the feeling that you are comfortable in this room if you actually are.

If you are the only one in this spot, it is still important to let your character start to come alive in the set. Start letting the character come to mind in your first few moments in the set. Get comfortable with it there. Run your lines there as soon as you can. Don't get in the way. Maybe you can run them while the crew is lighting or while they're taking a break. Just get the feeling of doing on the set the same dialogue and character you worked on at home.

Just as it was important to get the feel of doing this dialogue in wardrobe (or as close as you could come to it) at home, it is even more important to get used to delivering in the actual wardrobe. As soon as you are fitted with what you are to wear and the director and clients have approved it, try it out in the set.

If anything is going to be uncomfortable (i.e., getting out of a chair when the waist may be a bit tight, or maybe your shirt tail comes out when you have to reach high for that book, etc.) you're going to want to know about it early and do something about it. (Wardrobe could loosen the waist a little or give you a longer shirttail or hook it down with elastic [they can get very creative].)

If you wait until the last minute to find these things out, there may not be time to get them fixed and you will just have to deal with it. Why make it harder on yourself? Plan ahead a little bit, take care of as many problems as you can during rehearsal, and you'll have nothing to worry about during your performance except your performance.

Kids and Dogs

Rehearsing with kids and dogs can be great fun or occasionally a real trial. Since no one really knows for sure what a child or animal is going to do, it doesn't matter how much experience you've had—in this situation, you're going to be the steady one. Know up front that you are going to be relied upon.

Know also that you're going to be working a little harder to earn your money this time, but there are ways to help the shoot run smoothly.

This also is like meeting for the first time someone your character is supposed to be close to. You will have to get acquainted fast. It's even more important in this case, and you'll soon see why.

I think you'll find that most movie animals are easier to work with than movie kids because they're better trained. You show a movie dog a couple of times what you want him to do, give him a treat, and he'll deliver for you all day. Children don't quite work that way.

How hard you are going to have to work (or not) with animals will depend on how close you are supposed to be. If you want a movie dog to lick your face, no problem. A little honey will do the trick. They'll follow you around with a simple command, jump in and out of cars, pick up the paper, whatever. You don't have to worry about that.

If, however, this is your inseparable dog, good ol' dog that has been with you through thick and thin, your best friend in life, you're going to have to invest some time. But it will pay off in spades.

The dog will sit where it's supposed to and basically do what it's supposed to, but there's not going to be any love in its eyes if it just met you. There's no command for love.

If there is supposed to be a special bond between you and this dog, you've got to put one there. With the trainer (or at least with his permission), play with the dog. Throw a ball for him or Frisbee or whatever the dog really enjoys doing. Have the trainer let you give the dog treats every once in a while. If a dog knows you have treats, he'll be looking at you much differently, with much more attention and warmth than if you had not invested the time.

A good person-dog relationship photographs beautifully. Waiting until you are in front of the camera will be too late. It's got to be set up before. Do your best to make it happen. It will be noted and appreciated.

Much of the above relates to children as well. Many of these movie kids are quite bright. They might be able to do their lines all day and not miss a beat, but like the dog, there's going to be no love in their eyes if they have just met you.

If you are supposed to be very close and the intent of the spot depends on that closeness showing through, it is imperative for you to get to know the child. Find out what the child enjoys. What makes them smile? Parents always bring toys and/or games along to shoots to keep the kids from going crazy with boredom between shots. Play some of these games with them. Maybe you could color together?

Whatever it is, do it! Play hide and seek, dust off that old magic trick you haven't done in years. Pull a quarter out of her ear. Get the child laughing. Have fun.

The time you spend offstage with a child you're going to work with will make your on-camera time so much more alive that you won't believe it. Even if you're not speaking on camera, if a small child knows that you may pull a toy frog out of your pocket and bite her on the nose with it *at any moment*, just imagine how bright and alive her eyes will be, as opposed to a kid that you've never seen before, sitting in the car seat and everyone is trying to get the scene done quickly before she starts to cry again.

Most people working with kids on television are pretty good at it. Some aren't. Remember that KFC commercial I mentioned? Well, the final shot of that spot was with my "family" and me standing next to Harlan Sanders and smiling for the camera. (Harlan was actually the brother of the founder of KFC, but his likeness is the one we see everywhere. He also did their commercials for years.)

After a long day of riding that silly roller-coaster and eating chicken, everyone was ready to go home—especially the ten-year-old boy who played my son. He was standing directly in front of Harlan and was so tired he couldn't keep still. The director and I tried to get him to realize that if he could just force himself to stand still for a moment, it would all be over and he could leave. He kept squirming.

Suddenly, Harlan had had enough. He grabbed the boy by his shoulders and shook him strongly a couple of times and said in the nastiest voice he could muster, "Stand still! Don't you want to get paid?"

Mr. Sensitivity. It certainly woke the kid up, though, and scared him so much that he didn't move through two or three successful takes, after which we all were glad to be able to go home. Even though it worked, this is definitely not the approach to take if you are supposed to have any sort of relationship with a child.

Make rehearsal fun. Make it a game as much as you can. If a lot of takes are required, shooting might not be so enjoyable, but if the two of you have a recent history of playing together, that will help lighten the load immensely.

Depending on the script, you might even be able to carry over this playfulness into the actual shot. It might track just fine. Even if it doesn't, the relationship you've forged, even if it's just been in the last half-hour or so, will show in the child's eyes. Maybe in yours, too.

13

Acting on the Set

YOU NOW KNOW THE PRODUCT. YOU UNDERSTAND WHAT THE commercial is about. You know "the point" that the writer was trying to get across, and you've even rehearsed the way you are going to bring that point across. Now's the time to do it!

It amazes me that this even needs to be said, but be sure you know your lines when you show up in the morning. I am continually amazed at the number of actors who show up unprepared. I must also add that the work of these actors does reveal how much or how little they have put into their preparation. Needless to say, you will never find a veteran actor showing up unprepared.

Besides the obvious reason that knowing your lines is a basic part of your job, there are basic, commonsense reasons to do it. The main one is that knowing your lines gives you one less thing to worry about.

When you are starting a new shoot, you're meeting new cast, crew, and clients and getting used to a new set. Why burden yourself with having to get your lines down while you are also having to deal with everything else? It doesn't make sense.

Learn them in the tranquility of your home so that all you'll have to worry about on the set is your performance.

Another reason for advance preparation is that it makes you an instant hero. Ad agencies and clients, by their very nature, are a nervous lot. You have no idea how much commiserating went on behind closed doors before they finally decided to cast you. Now they are nervously hoping they made the right decision. Prove to them that they did.

If you show up prepared that first morning, everyone will breathe a sigh of relief and you'll find you have a whole group of people firmly on your side.

FLEXIBILITY ABOVE ALL

Do not confuse preparation with inflexibility. Know that filming this spot is going to be different from the audition, different from the callback, and different from the way you've been rehearsing it in your living room. Exactly how it's going to be different, nobody knows. Not even the director at this point. No one.

The reason is that a film set has its own dynamic. It is created by bringing together a script, actors, a director, and crew, many of whom have never even met each other before. But they all have their own creative contributions to make, and all will affect the outcome of the eventual commercial.

A lot of different viewpoints come into play, a lot of different agendas, abilities, and personalities. How well everyone works together and the extent of their vision and skill will determine the extent of the commercial's success.

Be prepared when you show up for work, and then be prepared for anything!

BEING NATURAL AND REAL

Occasionally, the point of a commercial is that it is not real (i.e., broad farce, aliens, animation, etc.). Primarily, though, you will be asked to be very real. Since the identification factor with the audience is a very big consideration, naturalness is mandatory. Your ability to do their dialogue naturally is probably what got you cast in the first place.

Most commercial copy, as mentioned, is actually a series of little slices of life, little scenes. They are usually reality-based but with heightened emphasis on whatever they are selling, i.e., the man in the spot may be a bit more concerned about the ring in the bathtub than you would be. Or the spot on your husband's golf shirt may not ruin your whole day.

However, if that's the role, go for the realism of the scene (or the realism that it's based on) and play that. Sometimes you may have to look for it, but you'll find it.

KEYS TO SUCCESS

To make your filming go smoothly and to end the day with everyone happy, I would suggest striving for the following qualities.

Likability

Remember the attributes we talked about in "auditioning." They still apply here. There is just too much media accosting people from every direction. It's impossible to pay attention to everything. Viewers pick and choose what to let in. They will tune you out (mentally or physically) if they get bad feelings from you.

Identifiability

The client wants the audience to experience the same joy you are feeling at having whiter whites, the same total satisfaction that you feel having bought a Pontiac, etc. Make sure your feelings come out and are known, so they can share them.

This, incidentally, is one of the reasons you will never be truly angry in a commercial. You may be frustrated but not angry. People will identify with frustration and still like you. They may not if you are really mad.

Approachability

Face the job as "one of the people," not talking down to anyone. You are fortunate in that you have discovered this wonderful product. You feel even more fortunate in being able to share it with these people. These are your friends, and you are very pleased that you are able to help them. Come across as someone the audience feels they could talk to.

Trustworthiness

Nobody's going to believe a word you say if they don't feel they can trust you. Try not to be too slick. The stereotype here is the used-car salesman who will tell you whatever you want to hear in order to sell you a car. He'll say all the right things, but you don't trust him for a minute.

Don't be perfect; be real. Sincerely believe that people will be better off if they get the message you are bringing to them.

(This reminds me of a George Burns line. When asked the reason for his long success, he paused for a beat, then said, "Sincerity . . . if you can fake that, you've got it made.")

It's very easy to get caught up and bugged by little things. Maybe there's a phrase in the copy that you're having trouble with. Maybe someone is giving you attitude. You didn't sleep well last night. The set's awfully hot. You just broke up with your boyfriend.

Move these concerns aside. Put them away. Keep in mind the Big Picture. Why are you and everyone else there? What are you trying to accomplish? What is your role in this? What are they paying you for?

The way we can do that is by breaking out our actor's "fourth wall" and putting it around the set. As long as this shoot takes, this set is your world. You'll deal with everything else later. Right now, you're busy.

That is what a professional attitude is. That is the attitude that will get you established and keep you in this business for a long time.

Of course, everyone realizes you're not going to do everything perfect all the time, but that is the goal. The observations shared here are meant to help direct your intentions. In the end, your intent is what's going to define your accomplishments.

14

The Director

THE DIRECTOR IS THE CREATIVE BOSS OF THE SHOOT. THE clients and the producers are technically the bosses because they are the money people. They, however, hire the director to bring their thoughts and ideas to life on film. (Actually, the thoughts and ideas belong to the writer they hired, but by the time the commercial has gotten as far as casting, the concept fully belongs to the clients and producers.)

Once the director has been hired, he takes over the project. He oversees everything that has to do with filming.

Most directors are good at working with people and you'll enjoy them quite a lot. Occasionally you'll run into one who has an abrasive personality. It's not necessary that you like this person. What is necessary is that you listen very closely to what he (or she, of course) says.

Since directors are also very human, some will be able to explain what they want beautifully—others won't. Sometimes you're going to have to work at trying to get the concept they want you to relate. If that happens, don't go crazy. It just becomes part of your job.

One thing that will help considerably is not to listen so much to the director's words as to the concept that he is trying to get across. Since you've already gone through the casting process and callbacks, you have a good idea of what's going on. But fine-tuning will always be needed. If his concept seems a little different from what you had in mind, be sure you get *his* concept.

When in doubt, ask questions. The director is the right person to ask, and now is the time. Use your head on this one, though. Remember that the director is everybody's boss. He has a big responsibility and is the busiest person on the set.

If you happen to disagree with something the director tells you, it may be a good thing to keep it to yourself. If you do mention your point of view, do it in the spirit of trying to understand and trying to help. Do not argue! This is a good way to lose any possible goodwill you may have built up. Instantaneously, everyone on the set will regret having hired you and they won't make that mistake again.

STAYING FLEXIBLE

Don't think you're doing something wrong if the clients keep asking for different things. They usually will want to print a number of different approaches. It gives them more of a choice in editing. (Remember that they have bosses they have to answer to also! The more good film they have *in the can,* the more secure they are.)

In the nearly forty years that I've been doing this, I've never done a shoot where they have printed "take one" and left it at that, nor have I (or anyone else) ever done a spot for which, from the start, the director said, "Perfect! I wouldn't change a thing."

It's not going to happen. They have to earn their money, too. Even if what you are doing is perfect, they'll try to make it better, or at least different. A good director is always going to try things. Everything isn't going to work, but some of it will. Your job is to go along with him. Whatever he wants to try, give it to him. Try to make it work. The result may be a reading that neither one of you had even anticipated!

FINE-TUNING

Know that in the course of a shoot, the director will always be tweaking—that is, making a lot of little changes. He wants you to put a little more emphasis on this word, romance that word a little more, slow it down a little, make it lighter, keep it slow but give it more energy, etc. There are always a lot of little shadings that the director will have you do.

Many people have all-or-nothing temperaments. It may be suggested to them that they are a little too nice in their reading. Next thing you know, all warmth is totally gone. Then the director goes crazy. "No, don't lose *all* of it!"

If you've ever played golf, use that as an analogy. When you're given instruction on your swing, the instructor is usually talking in tiny, tiny increments: 1/16th of a movement here results in a fifty-foot change two hundred yards down the fairway.

Same thing here. Remember, you got the job by being close to what they had in mind. Changes now are done very subtly. Ten percent more of this, twenty percent less of that. Use the performance in your callback as the basis, then build, change, or tweak as the director directs.

Sometimes the changes desired are so subtle that the mere mention of what they want you to do will be enough. You might just have to think "a little more smile in the voice" or "let a little more pride in the product show" in order for it to happen. These adjustments are very small.

TIMING

Another aspect of filming that throws a lot of actors is timing. Since commercials are usually sixty or thirty seconds long, scenes within those commercials are even shorter. Everything the client wants filmed must fit into that time frame. As such, everything has to be timed down to the half-second.

You may realistically get the direction to "trim it by a second and a half. You're a little long." Don't panic. It can be done, and it's not even that difficult. (It's only difficult if you make it that way.) We are indeed talking subtleties here. Actually, this may be another case where merely thinking about doing it just a tiny bit faster may be enough to actually do it.

I would try it that way first. If that doesn't do it, then just pick up the pace by taking ten percent from the rate of delivery you were doing before. Shorten some of the spaces between words. If you had taken a breath or made a small pause before a certain word to give it emphasis, try emphasizing it in another way that doesn't require a hesitation. Removing one hesitation may take care of the problem.

If the director wants you to cut three or four seconds out of a read (which in a commercial is a considerable amount of time) you'll just have to pick up your entire reading speed. Try different speeds until you get close, then use the little subtleties mentioned above to fine-tune it in.

It's much easier to stretch out a performance than to cut one. If you are short of the allotted time, you will have more time to play with the copy. You can milk key words, romance certain ideas, and put more natural pauses between words and sentences.

The temptation you must avoid here is to lose energy. When you slow something down it's natural to become a bit more laid back as you do it.

If a mellow attitude fits with the point of the spot, then fine, go with it. If it doesn't, you may have to consciously work to keep the intensity in your voice and manner while still delivering the words at a slower pace. (Think something like *deliberate* or *emphatic*. These are both strong, intense feelings that work best when done slowly.)

Above all, try not to be thrown by direction. It's given to help you. If it gets confusing, ask questions. If ideas seem contradictory to you, aim for the middle. If the director doesn't like it, he'll tell you which side to concentrate on and you've got the direction you need.

(Very seldom will you be asked to do something totally opposite of what you did in the callback. If you are, it's probably because the director would just like to try something different. If so, go for it. Trying wildly different things can sometimes turn out to be the most fun you'll have in acting. It may not work for what you're trying to do, but it's still fun. Never be afraid to give something like that a try.)

THE GOAL? PERFECTION

If the director is on his second hour of watching you coat your ribs with Carlson's Famous BBQ Sauce and you're wondering what it is that he's looking for, what he's looking for is perfection. Remember the big picture again. Hundreds of thousands of dollars and the jobs of many people have gone into this project before you came on the scene.

The result of the commercial you're doing may determine a large part of this product's future, which in turn impacts many, many more lives and even more dollars.

That's an awful lot to be riding on thirty or sixty seconds. So forgive them all if you feel that they are doing something to death. They may be. They're going for perfection.

It probably wouldn't hurt to think of your future at times like these. Good directors are always working. The film community isn't that large. If you stay in the business a while, you will keep running into people you've worked with in the past. The longer you stay in the business, the more you'll run into.

The work you have done, the images and impressions you have left behind, will follow you. Make sure they're good ones. What we're talking here, basically, is the difference between a four-year and a forty-year career.

This is an area where you can think of this job as an audition for the next, because, basically, that's what it is. If you do good work and the director enjoyed working with you, he will be predisposed to want to hire you again. It's just as simple as that.

A perfect illustration of this point happened to me a few years ago when I filmed a commercial with kids and a dog. The dog was totally preoccupied with his trainer and wouldn't take his eyes off him, and the kids were cute but were spoiled, cranky little brats. My job (as "Dad") was to do the spot and make us all read like a tight, loving family at the same time.

This was not a particularly big commercial, and I remember thinking that I wasn't being paid enough for that day. It wasn't much fun, just a lot of hard work (trying to get love, ease, and familiarity to read out of that bunch), but we got it done. Sometimes they're like that. The director recognized the work and time I was putting in with my "family," though, and was very appreciative.

A few weeks later, I auditioned for the "Sure" deodorant spot I mentioned earlier. This was the start of their massive "Raise your hand if you're Sure" campaign. Guess who the director was? You got it.

All I had to do was pretend to putt, then raise my hand in smiling, confident victory. That's it. Ten seconds. Anybody could have done it. As direct payback for the work I'd done for little money, he threw me a bone.

This particular bone took about two hours to shoot and was cut into six or seven different vignette spots. These all ran nationally for more than three years, making it one of the most lucrative spots I ever did.

Needless to say, I'm a firm believer in keeping the director happy.

CHAPTER

15

The Spokesperson

THE SPOKESPERSON HAS BEEN THE MAINSTAY OF COMMERCIALS since they first began and had a rather rudimentary beginning. A man or woman would hold or stand next to the product and talk about it. Period! A far cry from the extremely high-tech spots of today.

Some attributes of these original spots, however, are as necessary today as they were fifty years ago. We'll get into them in this chapter.

A sponsor can take a number of different commercial approaches to try to get information about his product across to the viewer. There are story commercials, slice of life, comedy, hard sell, travelogues, games, contests, sales, and of course, sometimes they just have someone standing next to the product talking about it.

The spokesperson is the conveyer of knowledge and good news. Many of the commercial approaches listed above are still spearheaded by a spokesperson. Our job as spokesperson is basically to direct the viewer's attention where the sponsor would like it to go.

We point out how tangy and wonderful Carlson's famous BBQ sauce is and direct the viewers to try it for themselves. We point out "Corinthian Leather seats" and "no aftertaste" and "money-back guarantees" and make sure you grasp the full significance of squeezable toilet paper.

We may laugh about it sometimes, but it would be good for us to remember that advertising the world's products is a multibillion-dollar-a-year business, and the spokesperson is right in the middle of it.

INTO THE LENS

Since every career is unique and individualistic, an actor never knows for sure exactly where his acting career may take him. You may never be given the instruction of looking into the lens even once. If your career encompasses commercials, however, I can promise you that looking into the lens is something with which you'll want to become very comfortable.

That's where the spokesperson is, right in front of the camera, looking into the lens, talking to the viewers of the land like they were old friends.

Some of the attributes of the spokesperson that haven't changed over the years are naturalness, believability, and authority. Whatever you are called upon to do in a commercial, you must do it in such a convincing way that viewers believe you. That's the basic given.

When people watch someone on TV, what they look at primarily are the eyes. If you, as a spokesperson, are looking into the lens, talking directly to those watching, you are looking them in the eyes as well.

So here you are, looking at the viewer eye to eye, talking about this product, and your job is simply to make sure they believe you.

If what you do on camera does successfully get the point across to the extent that the client sees a difference in sales, your commercial will have a long, healthy life and your bank account will reflect that success.

Look Away

I mentioned the effectiveness of "looking away" from the lens in auditioning to give the impression of ease and security. Well, now that we're doing it for keeps, it's even more important. Staring at the lens constantly is like looking someone in the eyes constantly. People don't do that. It comes across as unreal.

The more you can look away from the camera (copy permitting, of course) the less you will appear to be an actor on television selling a product. By looking away from the lens (or, one of my favorites, starting the spot looking away, then coming into the camera), you are implying a life, an involvement with something other than the lens.

This adds to the feeling of sharing something rather than selling something. Sharing is nicer, gentler, and since all commercials try to create a positive feeling about their product, it usually is received very well.

Sometimes being a spokesperson entails dealing with huge amounts of dialogue. Fortunately, for these big chunks, there exists an over-the-lens teleprompter. If you do much work at all as a spokesperson, you will get to know this marvelous apparatus intimately.

Even though your words will now appear to you over the lens, the performance you give still has to have all the freedom and naturalness that it would have if the teleprompter wasn't there. We'll get into that in the next chapter. There are enough considerations in dealing with the prompter and cue cards that this entire chapter is devoted strictly to them.

BEING, NOT ACTING

Many times as an actor you'll be dealing with the difference between "acting" like someone and "being" that someone. A clear example (even though it's one you will never use in a commercial) is dealing with being drunk. If you were told to act like you were drunk, you might slur your speech and be a little unsteady on your feet.

If you were directed to BE drunk, that would be different, because a drunken person practically always will try not to act drunk. They still may be unsteady and their speech still may slur, but their subtext, their intent, is to act like they are not drunk.

In the depiction of a drunk it's also much more interesting to see the person trying hard to act sober while the drunkenness seeps out anyway.

Okay, so how do we incorporate that example into commercials? The answer is the actor's Point Of View (POV). Who are you, and why are you telling the viewer these things about this product?

If your POV is as an actor trying to read your lines as effectively as possible, your performance will be paper-thin and people will see right through you.

If your POV is as an intelligent, caring, competent person who wants to share something that will make the viewer's life better, you're going to get more people's attention.

Be that caring person as you walk into the set. Be that person before the camera rolls, then do your copy as that person (that aspect of you) would do it.

The viewer must trust you. This is not a time to get caught acting. Keep your performance as honest and simple as you can. That's what will work for you.

PRIDE

As I've pointed out, looking directly into the lens, as you are in most spokesperson situations, reveals many subtle feelings and emotions that might be harder to convey in, say, a slice-of-life scene.

One emotion that shines through is pride. We can help this along by placing it in the forefront of our consciousness. Be very proud of your association with this product and let it show. (Just like drunkenness, let it creep out.)

Have you ever noticed how many CEOs are doing commercials for their companies? They do them for one reason: they work! CEOs are not actors. They are not particularly polished as performers, but they are totally devoted to their product. No one believes in the product more than the CEO who puts himself and his reputation on the line to come on television, look you in the eye, and ask you to try his product because it's excellent and he knows you will love it.

Your tip: act like that CEO. Have your pride in this product (*your* product) be that real. Let that pride shine through. You couldn't hide it if you wanted to. That's how strongly you feel about this product.

When you are watching TV, notice when a spokesperson comes on that you feel is really effective. Why? What are they doing that's working? I'll bet one of the attributes you'll find is that they are totally dedicated to their product. You believe them!

Singleness of purpose and thought reads very strongly. (Could anybody be better at selling Tony Robbins' tapes and seminars than Tony Robbins? He's a great example of total singleness of purpose.) When you are on the set, view your product and copy with that same determination.

The enthusiasm you feel is, of course, tempered by the fact that you are talking to a close friend (otherwise, you'd be shouting it from the rooftops!). Enthusiasm, like pride, is something else you want to let seep out on its own. It's much more effective to let the viewers notice this, rather than hitting them over the head with it.

SPOKESPERSON SUMMARY

More than you will do in any other type of commercial, as a spokesperson you really will represent the product. As such, it is even more important to be identifiable, likable, and trustworthy. Those are the attributes the client hired you for. To the extent that you can deliver them, the client will be happy with the shoot.

The more comfortable you can make yourself in the shooting surroundings, the better. Comfort comes across on film as naturalness, which is another prime ingredient of a successful spokesperson.

16

Teleprompter and Cue Cards

AS FAR AS I'M CONCERNED, THE PERSON WHO INVENTED THE teleprompter should be nominated for sainthood, or at least knighted. It's the most helpful aid for the actor since the invention of the microphone.

What it is, basically, is a television-type unit hooked to the front of the camera that reflects your dialogue onto a slanted pane of glass in front of the lens. Because of the slant, the camera looks right through the glass, seeing nothing. You, however, while looking at the lens actually see your dialogue reflected there on the glass, plain as day.

This chapter is sort of a companion piece to the "Spokesperson" chapter, since this type of teleprompter, obviously, can only be used when you are looking straight into the lens. It allows you to talk on and on about most anything and not miss a beat. Politicians can look the viewer in the eye and talk for hours about what a great job they're doing and never miss a point. It's wonderful.

The teleprompter does have a couple of drawbacks, actually more like a couple of things to be aware of. Because of its size, the over-the-lens prompter can't be on the camera all the time. If the camera has to make any sudden moves, it has to come off because of its weight. Weight also prohibits it from being used for crane shots. If the camera has to get into a small space, it has to come off because of its size. If the actor is too far away from the camera to read it, the teleprompter doesn't do any good and just gets in the way.

Of course, a teleprompter is never used with anything handheld because it's too heavy and cumbersome, and it's no good for straight acting work because you don't want to be looking into the lens during a scene.

Figure 16–1 Side view of teleprompter. *(Photo courtesy of Jim Estochin Teleprompting.)*

So, it can't be used for everything. But for what it *can* be used for, it's wonderful. Let's learn how to deal with it.

TIPS FOR USING A TELEPROMPTER

The fact that they are using a teleprompter at all shows that you have a lot of dialogue and the director isn't even going to ask you to try to memorize it all. That makes most actors emit a sigh of relief. Now you don't have to concentrate so much on remembering the words and instead can work on your delivery.

You should still make every effort to get the script as soon as possible, and even though you don't have to memorize it, you should still be very comfortable with it. Make sure you understand the various points you'll be making. Make sure there aren't any strange words that you don't understand or know how to pronounce.

Also remember that changes on a film set occur constantly. Something may come up that will require taking the prompter off for a particular shot. You would then have to memorize at least a part of the script, so the more familiar you are with it, the easier time you'll have dealing with the problems and exceptions that come up.

When you arrive for work in the morning, the first thing you should do after greeting the director and clients is to introduce yourself to the teleprompter operator. This person should be your new best friend by the time you start shooting. If you are going to do a great job in this spot, you are going to have to work very closely and well with this person.

After introducing yourself to the operator and letting him know what a fine person you are, you should both go over the script. Make sure that what is down on the prompter is the same as the script with which you've become familiar. If not, run it by the director and/or the script supervisor. They will work out any discrepancies. If that means a change for you, you've now found out about it first thing in the morning and have plenty of time to become comfortable with it before shooting.

By the time you are standing in front of the camera and teleprompter, there should be no surprises regarding dialogue.

Reading Without Letting It Show

This is another situation where it's necessary for you to be a good reader. Unlike reading off a cue card while auditioning, when everyone knew you were reading, here, if you look or act like you are reading, it totally defeats the purpose.

I'll give you some tips that will help you convince people that you are not reading (even though you are), which will help a lot. Nothing, however, will do any good if you are not a good reader.

Remember the exercise about how to check yourself for acting? Now, do the same thing when you are reading. Whether you are speaking normally to someone or reading something out loud, there should be no difference in your voice. The speed with which you speak, your pitch, inflection, everything should be the same.

You're looking the viewers in the eyes. You want them to believe that you are this character in your commercial. You have to pull that off while also having them not become aware that you are reading your lines. (What was that part again about how commercials weren't real acting?)

Don't let me scare you. It's not really all that difficult. I just wanted to underline the importance of being a good, natural reader. If you're not, all of this becomes *very* difficult.

The best way to learn to read aloud, by the way, is to read aloud. Practice. Do it at home. A newspaper is perfect. Stand and sight-read the newspaper. Read only as fast as you can while saying everything smoothly and steadily. Don't go fast on one-syllable words and slow down on four-syllable words. Keep it smooth.

You might be fairly slow at first, but don't worry about it. You will be amazed at how much faster you'll get with just a little bit of practice. You'll soon find that you are reading in your mind, further ahead of the words that you are speaking.

That ability right there is what's going to enable you to read aloud as naturally as you speak.

REHEARSING WITH THE PROMPTER

The reason it's so important to get to know the prompter operator is that you're going to be spending so much time together. Also, in order for you to have a smooth, natural delivery, the operator has to understand and be comfortable with your timing.

These operators are normally pretty good. All you have to do is show them how to work with you.

The operator sits at a desk or table not far off the set. He (or she) has a monitor in front of him that is the same as the prompter set attached to the camera. He sees what you see. On the face of the prompter, to the side of the dialogue, is a movable arrow.

This arrow points to the line you are currently speaking. You can have it adjusted anywhere you want. It's up to you. Where do you want the line you are speaking to be on the face of the prompter? Personally, I like mine to be a quarter to a third of the way down from the top. (The dialogue travels from bottom to top, by the way.) That way I never seemed rushed to get out the line before, and I have plenty of room to read ahead in my mind. It also makes it easier for me to choose pauses.

Try some placements to see what seems good and comfortable to you, then practice with the prompter operator. When you are comfortable with each other's timing off the set, it's time to try it on the camera.

When rehearsing with the camera and prompter, it's important to practice it as you are going to be shooting it. If you are walking or moving at all, try to get as much rehearsal as possible with the camera going through all the moves you are both going to be making in the actual scene.

There are a couple of other things you should be aware of here. The teleprompter and operator are there for only one reason, and that is to help you handle this dialogue. That's it! So feel free to rehearse as long and as many times as you want. The operator is there for you. All you have to do is mention what you need, and he will be glad to comply.

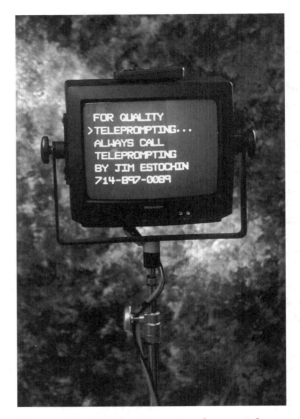

Figure 16-2 Teleprompter face with arrow. (*Photo courtesy of Jim Estochin Teleprompting.*)

On the other hand, the camera crew has many considerations other than you. It is not their job to rehearse anytime you want. They'll usually give you one or two rehearsals before shooting, but that's it. If you get more, it's mainly because something is not right with the shot and as long as they have to continue rehearsing the camera moves, you can also have the prompter running.

If there's enough dialogue to merit having a prompter, you should be looking for as much rehearsal time with it as possible. You'll have to be alert and look for opportunities.

Sometimes while everyone is taking five and the camera is left in the set, you can have the operator run the prompter just to get the practice of reading it off the camera unit.

Or many times I've seen the camera crew going through their moves in the set with my stand-in while lighting. I've jumped in, excused my stand-in, taken his place and got a chance to practice my prompted dialogue, with camera moves, while they are lighting me.

(They always appreciate lighting the actual actor anyway, so as long as you remember that this is basically their time and you're there to help them [not the other way around] everyone should be pleased, and you have managed to get a little extra rehearsal time.)

LOOK AWAY

In a prompted spot, you are going to be acting while making it look like you are not acting, and you are going to be reading while making it look like you are not reading.

What they're generally looking for is the steady, easy, natural read I've been mentioning but if you really want to convince the viewer that you are not reading, I'd suggest dusting off a little trick that I mentioned in the Auditioning portion of this book. Look away.

By this time, you should be very familiar with the dialogue. Look for a place where you could conceivably look away. The most obvious, of course, is to look over at the product as you mention it. (This won't work if you are talking about a mutual fund, but it sure could if you're talking about how clean your floors are or about your new car parked outside.)

There is a little arrow on the teleprompter face that marks where in the dialogue you are reading. You can use that arrow to show you exactly where you are when you come back to the camera.

Also remember that you can begin the spot by looking off camera, then look into the lens and begin your dialogue or (subject matter permitting, of course) even start speaking before you turn into the camera.

All of these techniques belie the fact that you are reading, and they're all effective. Give them a try.

WORKING WITH CUE CARDS

The main place you are likely to run into cue cards anymore is in auditioning. Even though they are cheap and easy to use, they really don't have much application for commercials. Spokespeople are usually the only ones with copious amounts of dialogue. Cue cards can't help them much because they can't be placed over the lens. They have to be placed next to it. As such, the actor's look is pulled off to one side of the lens, which shows glaringly.

Cards can be used well, if necessary, during scene shooting because they can be placed around the set in the actor's line of vision, not on the camera. They are used in this capacity in soap operas quite a lot because the actors have so much dialogue to deal with on a daily basis, but commercials hardly ever have that much dialogue, being only thirty to sixty seconds long.

PROBLEMS WITH CUE CARDS

But what if problems arise and you have to use cards? Well, sometimes you just have to get creative.

If you are in a spokesperson situation without a prompter (it does happen) and the words just are not sticking in your brain (that does, too), they may decide to make some cards on the set. The problem here, of course, is that you will be looking off to one side. How best to minimize this?

First of all, maybe you don't need to have all the dialogue given to you, but instead you just need a transition or help getting over a particularly rough part. Could you look away there? If you could work a look-away into the performance at that point, you could have the cards placed right where you would be looking.

If not, another approach could be to have the camera moved back away from you. They can put on another lens to shoot you as close as before, even with the camera moved back. Have the cards written only as big as they have to be for you to read them. Also, use only half of the card—the half closest to the lens.

Because of the distance, your glance to the side won't be nearly as noticeable. Even so, when you finish reading, don't look back over into the lens. Hold your look at the bottom of the card. If it's so-o-o close, many times, viewers won't even notice that you're not looking directly into the lens. But if you look back and forth, you will reveal exactly what you're doing and they will immediately know you're reading.

If you only needed help with the first part of the script and had the second part memorized, the only way you can come back to the camera (in the same shot) is to look away. If you do that, then come back into the lens and deliver the rest of the dialogue, it should work just fine. (It's just the ping-ponging back and forth that doesn't work.)

If the camera cannot be moved far away, have the cards written as small as they can possibly be while still enabling you to read them, and have them placed as close to the lens as possible.

If you do need cards in a scene situation, the cards can be placed just off your line of vision. (Again, don't dart your eyes back and forth from cards to person because you'll give it away.)

Another really sneaky maneuver, when you're very close to the camera and need the cards, is to cut down a card to about twelve by seven inches. Cut a hole in the middle of the card just big enough to fit the lens through it, and let it sit there. Part of your words will then be above the lens (written as small as possible) and part below. This is certainly not the best way to do things, but it has been known to work.

PROBLEMS WITH THE TELEPROMPTER

Sometimes situations occur that make it tough to use a prompter effectively. However, because they are all computerized, changes and adaptations can be handled quickly and easily.

Let's say the camera is in an extreme close-up of you. Being this close, it can see your eyes going back and forth as you are reading off the prompter. What to do? Easy. It's a computer, remember? And these operators are good.

All you have to do is ask the operator to bring the font size down as small as they can while still allowing you to read it. Then have them bring the sides of the text in so that they don't extend beyond the size of the lens. (The lens can be seen faintly behind your words, incidentally.) You can then read the whole thing right in front of the lens, and your eyes will hardly move at all.

If you want to get outrageously good at this, you can even practice using your peripheral vision while reading. By doing this, you will cut down on your eye movement whenever you are reading from the prompter.

Most people usually won't pick up on what you are doing. What they'll do is say things like "Boy, you're good," but they won't know why.

Just say, "Thank you."

THE "EAR"

Another way to have your lines fed you, and one that is considerably cheaper than a teleprompter, is to use a little device called the "ear." (I mentioned it in Chapter 10.)

The ear is a unit about the size of a hearing aid that is tuned to the same frequency as a tape recorder unit in your back pocket, or jacket pocket, purse, etc. On this tape, you have recorded all your dialogue, with all the inflections and timing you want for your performance.

What you do then, is play it back. As soon as you hear yourself say something, you will mimic what you said, in exactly the same way: same pauses, same inflections, everything.

It sounds difficult, but some actors become very good at it. Being much cheaper than a teleprompter, the ear is especially popular for use in industrial films where there's usually a lot of dialogue and a small budget. (Teleprompters with trained operators can get pretty expensive.)

As in auditioning, even in shooting, the main drawback in using an ear is that it's hard to make changes. If the director wants you to speed up your pace a little, or slow it down, or the client decides to change the dialogue somewhat or would like you to try a few different things, everything has to wait while you reprogram your tape, and time is the most expensive commodity on a film set.

Just like teleprompters or cue cards, no tool works for every purpose, but for the right situations, the ear can come in quite handy.

CHAPTER

17

Attitude on the Set

YOU MAY BE SURPRISED THAT I CONSIDER ATTITUDE IMPORTANT enough to devote two chapters to it. Actually, it could probably stand more. How you face this work and all that goes with it will be extremely important. Many times, the type of career you are going to have (or not have) depends on your attitude toward it.

ALWAYS BE PART OF THE SOLUTION

In my professional life, I have seen so many young, talented actors and actresses, who should have had long, lucrative careers, burn themselves out very quickly because of attitude.

When you are shooting a commercial, you are an integral part of the team. Some people's job is to write the spot, others to film it, and yours happens to be to say the words. Nobody can exist without the others.

Sometimes problems happen. The director and clients have a lot to deal with. The ability to make your part of the equation one area that they don't have to worry about is one that will help you more than you know.

When you think about it, shooting commercials is quite a varied field and to be successful at it, it would be wise to be aware of its many facets. You're dealing with the technicalities of auditioning, of filmmaking, of portraying the honesty of a good acting performance, of sales and marketing, plus the psychology of working closely and well with people from all walks of life, most of whom you've never met before.

Please—never, ever try to play star in a commercial. First of all, you will impress no one. Remember, these people work with actors every day. They know who's a star and who isn't. Besides, as far as these people are concerned, you're not the star anyway, the product is! You don't want to be the only one who doesn't know that.

Also, the "powers that be" can replace you in a minute. (Remember all those people you auditioned with? Well, someone came in second, and I can promise you, they still have that actor's phone number.)

AN ASIDE

I just thought of a story about an incident I got a big kick out of a few years ago that shows the human side of ad agency folks.

I was shooting a ten-second tag for Star-Kist Tuna. This tag showed a typical American family sitting around a table eating, and would be placed at the end of the Charlie Tuna cartoon commercials that they ran for years. (Needless to say, it was a good account.)

I remember the ad agency people on this shoot seemed to have less humor and be a bit more uptight than most. Here we were, making a tag for a cartoon, and these people acted as though we were shooting *War and Peace*.

One time, while heading for the coffee machine, I happened to pass one of the most serious of the lot, all buttoned up in his gray three-piece suit. What I saw made me laugh out loud before I could catch myself. This uptight "suit" was wearing a *Charlie Tuna tie!* It was dark blue with smiling Charlie Tunas all over it.

He, of course, wondered why I was laughing at him. I mentioned that I had never seen a Charlie Tuna tie before and thought it was great. In an extremely serious tone of voice, he asked if I would like one. Not really knowing what else to say, I said that I would love to have a Charlie Tuna tie. He said "Fine. We have your address on the contract. We'll send you one."

I thanked him very much and returned to the other actors, knowing that I would never actually see the tie. (Lots of people say lots of things. Unfortunately, most don't follow through.)

A few weeks later I was amazed to get a package in the mail, containing not only my very own Charlie Tuna tie (which I still have) but also a *Charlie Tuna Watch!* (How many people do you know who have one of *those*?)

Not only was the ad agency guy honorable (he did what he said he was going to do and more), but he might have had some humor in there after all.

Anyway, I thought it was terrific and appreciated it a lot.

Back to business. I don't think I would have gotten my tie and my watch (let alone have been hired in the first place) if I had been difficult to work with.

WORD GETS OUT

There's also a very basic, pragmatic reason to make yourself a delight to work with and that is the fact that the world of commercials is actually a very small community. People know each other. Word gets out.

Some people get hot, famous, and rich, while others never work again. People talk. It doesn't take long for the good ones to get found out. It takes even less time for the bad ones.

You have more control than you may think over the length and success of your career.

PROFESSIONALISM

We keep coming back to it, don't we? The dictionary defines a *professional* as one who is skilled, capable, expert, trained, able, and adept. All of those definitions lead to one thing: *confidence* in this person and in his or her abilities.

Make that person *you*.

In case I didn't make myself clear earlier, I'm not suggesting that you try to make everybody like you. You're going to be working together too short a period of time for that. What you want to strive for is to have people like working with you; there's a big difference. (There may not be enough time on a shoot for people to know whether they legitimately like you, but there is plenty of time for them to tell if they *don't* like you.)

The set is a wonderful training ground. Keep your eyes open. Watch how people interact. See what's effective and what isn't. See what's appreciated and what isn't. Learn from others.

File away the traits of people who are more experienced or more successful than you. What are they doing that you aren't? What can you learn from that? Also pay attention to the mistakes others make. There's no sense in making them yourself.

Some basic guidelines to professionalism are listed below:

- Never be late.
- Never keep production waiting for you.
- Be fully prepared and ready before you walk onto the set.
- Be calm, quiet, and attentive around the set.
- Acquire as soon as you can a good understanding of the process of filmmaking. Know (learn) what's going on around you.
- Pick the time to tell your favorite joke carefully. While you are on the set is probably not the time.
- Always be available for rehearsal. Help your fellow actors as much as possible.
- Treat everyone with courtesy and respect.

Blended with the above, the most important thing for you to do that will make and keep everybody happy with you is to simply do a bang-up job with their spot. Don't get involved with extracurricular drama. Keep your focus, and handle yourself with the professionalism of a professional actor, and you'll do fine.

REALITY CHECK

Of course, I know this advice is easy to give but sometimes hard to follow. On your first few jobs, you may be so nervous that you have to work hard at keeping your lines straight. Some days you may not feel well.

There are many variables that enter the picture. What I'm giving you with these professional guidelines is what your intentions should be. These are your goals.

Don't beat yourself up if you fall short sometimes. I can promise you that it's going to happen. Your intent here is to learn from your mistakes, to file them away in your consciousness so as never to make the same mistake again, and then let it go. Again, this is much easier said than done, but still necessary to do.

One basic necessity for acting like the professional you want to be (on and off camera) is to think of yourself in that vein. Even if it's one of your first few jobs, you are the hired professional there, so act like it. Come from that point of view.

Intend always to make professional excellence an integral part of your self-image.

CHAPTER

18

The Business of the Business, Part 2

BY THE TIME YOU'VE REACHED THIS POINT IN THE BOOK, YOU might already be working. You've learned some helpful hints along the way, and I hope you are putting them to good use. You've certainly learned what to expect. Minimizing surprises is always good.

As this book winds down, let's deal with what happens next. You've started to work. What you want to do now is to turn these first few commercial jobs into a full-blown career.

What follows are a number of points I feel are crucial for building a successful career in show business (and not just commercials).

NOTHING IS FOREVER

How many times have you heard stories about actors who were on a hit TV series, or who made a string of movies and seemed destined for stardom, only to be dead broke and ruined a few years later?

What happened? What happened was that they didn't plan for the future. If we're on top of the world for a moment, it's tempting to think that it will always be that way. Wrong.

As the title of this section says, "Nothing is forever." The only constant in this business is change, and not all change is for the better. Life is constantly in a state of flux, either going up or down but always moving.

As long as you realize that, you can have a rather large say in which direction that change makes in your life. If you are not aware of it, you won't be able to prepare for it, and that casts your future not only to the whim of the winds, but also leaves you vulnerable to others in the business who are aware of the situation and are doing their best to further themselves.

Let's see what we can come up with that would make the odds a little more favorable.

LIFE SETUP

We touched on this at the beginning of the book, but it's time to underline it again. Setting up your life to complement what you are doing career-wise (or what you want to do) is not just a getting-started thing. It's a living happily ever after thing.

You saw what the pay scale for this industry is. Your first few jobs are probably not going to supply you with a living wage. For that reason, it may be good to think of a commercial career in its infancy as an interesting addition to a steadier job that can pay some bills.

Remember how debt and problems show. You can't just turn off emotions like that when you walk into an audition room (even if you think you can). There's a subtle desperation that shows. It comes across as weakness, and it will stop you from getting cast.

Keep your life as simple as possible. Stay out of debt. Let your lifestyle rise as your income rises. Give yourself a place to go. Don't give yourself everything you've ever wanted until you can pay for it.

Don't make yourself responsible for long-range debt (i.e., mortgages, car payments, etc.) until you are reasonably certain of your long-range income.

Having a house or a car repossessed, besides being outrageously embarrassing, is going to look horrible on your credit rating. This is going to make things harder for you when you can actually afford to get the things you were trying to get prematurely.

Being practical, realistic, and planning ahead can save you an awful lot of heartache down the road.

Some people try to embrace adversity. They have found that they can work the "poor me" syndrome to their benefit quite well. Well, they weren't in show business. "Relying on the kindness of strangers" may work in some circles, but it will not get you cast in anything! Especially not commercials. They want someone emitting health, security, and happiness, not someone to be pitied.

One of the points I'm trying to make here is that being healthy, confident, and happy is much more effective than trying to act like you are.

The more you can keep your life on a manageable, enjoyable level, the much better off you will be.

POLITICS

No, this is not a dirty word. What I'm referring to here is the science and fine art of dealing with people. This is a lot more important than many people think.

Consider for a moment how many thousands of people want to get into this business. Imagine how inundated casting directors and agents are with "hopefuls." In the beginning, you're competing with all of these people too. Until you have a body of work behind you, how do people already in the industry know that you are a legitimate contender for the job and not just another starry-eyed somebody?

A lot of the instruction you've been given already in this book has been designed to separate you from the crowd. The most effective way to do that, of course, is to know people. (Not to be known as the seventy-third actor to walk through the door on an audition, but to be known as you.) Relationships in this business are golden. Treat everyone you meet in this business with dignity and respect.

Never "burn your bridges." You can never tell for sure what's going to happen or who's going to make it happen. This year's secretary is next year's casting director. Life doesn't stand still for anyone.

Remember people's names. (People like that a lot.) If someone is nice to you or has helped you along in some way, thank them. If it was a big help, send flowers or a bottle of wine. If it was a little help, a card with a sincere "thank you" will do.

Send good wishes and considerations like these all the time, but don't actively expect to get something in return. It will happen, but you'll never know when and it may take a form you never expected. Don't limit it by expecting a certain response. Just be a polite, considerate person and let it go at that. Rewards will find their own way of reaching you.

Strive for excellence in every job you do, even if your first jobs are small ones. Your best insurance for the future is doing a good job now.

If you happen to get a good job theatrically (on TV or films) or are doing a play nearby, let the commercial people know. Send cards or fliers to casting directors and agents (if you don't have one yet) and especially be sure to notify the people you've worked with and those people I just mentioned who have helped you along the way.

Show business people are still "fans." We like to know people who are doing things. Also, if someone has helped you, they evidently thought you were worthy of it. I'm sure they don't go around helping everyone, so they must have thought you were special. Show them that their trust in you was justified.

This is also another way of separating yourself from the pack. Anybody can say anything, and in this business, many times they do. There are many more talkers than do-ers. Advertise. As soon as you have something to talk about—something real and tangible—call attention to it. Let it be known that you are a do-er.

LEARN FROM OTHERS' CAREERS

Life isn't all that changes. Since show business in general and commercials in particular are in the business of representing life, what goes on in the commercial world changes also. What "everyone" was doing last year might not make it this year. Stay on top of trends. You don't want to be seen as old-fashioned or out of step with what's happening today.

There is, however, a fine line between keeping up to date and becoming too trendy. You want to be perceived as an individual, not just another sheep, but you also want to be *au courant.*

Keep up to date, but also keep your own style.

Watch not only others' work but their careers as well. Why is actor "A" successful? Is there something you can learn here? Why is actor "B" not? Is there a lesson there as well?

Never forget the importance of getting and keeping a positive attitude (even when it's tough.). Singing the blues, griping, and being negative are the kiss of death to an acting career. Bitterness is practically impossible to hide.

Be confident and capable, not arrogant. Be what they are going to hire you for.

Be consistent as a person. When you are not auditioning or shooting something, be your professional, charming self. Be as good an actor as you can be while working, but don't be a chameleon when you are not.

Let people know who you are. Which you? How about the reliable-friendly-easy-to-get-along-with-and-easy-to-work-with you?

BUSINESS

Remember those broke movie stars? Try to learn something from their plight.

I think it's important to reward yourself for victories or for jobs well done, but keep them in perspective. If you've just finished a great job but don't have an ironclad contract for another year's worth of them, don't run out and buy yourself a new car. (Maybe buy a new sport coat or treat you and your significant other to a night on the town.)

Start building an IRA as soon as possible. Keep your monthly expenses down and try to have at least three months' rent and expenses in the bank. Then stretch that to six months. When you have accomplished that and the future still looks rosy, then it's time to move up.

Still, be careful: "Expect the best, but prepare for the worst."

Once you start making money, it's very important what you do with it. You're moving up but you're not all the way there yet. If possible, I'd start looking for a house or condominium. (Of the two, I personally would recommend a house if you can afford it. I prefer the aesthetics, and equity generally builds quicker.)

What this does is to let you own something. If you can come up with the down payment (and if you are adhering to the above formula, you should be able to) you can probably buy a house with monthly payments close to what you are paying for rent.

Rent is not tax deductible. House payments are. That fact alone makes it worth doing. Don't think you need to be older or married to buy a house. Not so. I was twenty-four years old and single when I bought my first one, and it turned out to be the best investment I've ever made.

(Remember that if you buy a car, it depreciates every day you own it. If you buy a house or condo and you've bought well, it appreciates every day you own it.)

Consider the possibility of becoming a homeowner. If your career is starting to take off, this might be the right time to talk with a real-estate agent.

(This advice is for women, too, please understand. My wife was a professional dancer for years and had the money to buy a house when she was young but didn't do it because "girls just weren't doing that." She's still kicking herself. Don't make that same mistake.)

OVEREXPOSURE

Let's take a quick look at a problem I hope you'll have: overexposure. Since the basis of commercials is to have you (your image, your persona) linked with the product, if you are doing a lot of spots and are seen all over the tube, clients are eventually going to feel that you don't bring the necessary specialness to their spot.

The same problem arises if you've done one or a series of spots that are hugely successful. If you are recognized as the actor in all of the national Carlson's BBQ Sauce ads, this is not going to help you get hired for Toyota.

At some point, you'll have to watch it. At the beginning of your career, take everything and shoot everything. You want people to see your work, and there's so much for you to learn. You need the practice.

Once you start doing national commercials, you'll want to be very careful about how many local spots you do. When clients or ad people watch television, they don't register whether the commercial they are watching is national, regional, or local. If you are seen often in local commercials, the client may feel you are overexposed. You, the casting director, and your agent will try to convince the client that you are not seen anywhere in the country except this one town so you shouldn't be considered overexposed at all.

But this is a business run a lot by gut instincts. You may have all the logic in the world on your side, but it just may not feel right to someone.

However, this can also work to your advantage. Let's say you are the new spokesperson for RCA. Bob's Auto Mart might think that having you appear in his local commercial might add some credibility and clout.

You have to plan how you are going to play it. There are many different approaches, and no two situations are exactly alike. The point here is that you are going to have to do something. There comes a time when you can't just blissfully take every job that comes along and think you are building a great career because you are working a lot.

What that creates is the equivalent of the broke-star syndrome. Think back over the years to some of the faces you used to see in commercials all the time. Where are they now? They might have overdone it.

Of course, you may decide to take the money and run. Shoot as much as you can! Do as much as you can while you're hot. That's okay, too. Just be aware of what you're doing. This can work well if you have another job or career that you can move into after commercials dry up for you.

It can be a great, fun ride. Realize, though, that if you want a long, professional career, you're going to have to put more thought into it than that.

Talk it over with your agents. They're not there only to get you interviews, you know. They are your advisors. Their job is to help you build as successful a career as you can. Career moves, what to do and what not to do, are very much a part of that.

Here's one parting thought:

How wonderful you are always means so much more when someone else says it.

CHAPTER

19

Commercials: The First Step to Stardom

WHEN YOU ARE STARTING OUT ON A NEW BUSINESS OR career, it's normal (and healthy) to want to go as far as you can. In a business as capricious and difficult as this one, you've got to give yourself every opportunity to succeed. Actors who think their commercial and theatrical careers have nothing to do with each other are, perhaps, unaware of how one can help the other.

Once you've become established in commercials, the income generated may help support a theatrical career in which you may not be as established. I draw your attention, once again, to the monetary figures at the beginning of the book. As you saw, it takes a lot of theatrical work to make a decent living. Income from commercials can help considerably.

May I also remind you of the seven-figure deals celebrities are making in the overseas commercial world?

Even so, the beginning of a career is probably the time when commercials can help the most. Everything you need to know to become a movie star (or at least a successful working actor) can be learned through the filming of commercials.

Consider the following points.

AUDITIONING

Although auditioning for spokesperson commercials is quite different from auditioning for TV or films, auditioning for scene-type spots is not. You and a partner are in a small room, pretending you're wherever you are supposed to be, saying the lines in the scene.

The fact that you are being videotaped instead of just watched (as in TV and features) doesn't really affect your audition. The way you handle both situations will be the same.

The more you involve yourself in the art of auditioning, the more comfortable and effective you will become, and that is very important. Auditioning nerves probably do more to stop actors from getting work than anything else.

If, through the commercial audition and casting process, you become less panicked at the concept of auditioning for a director and/or producer, you have taken a giant step forward and are already in a much better position than other actors at the same level who are not getting this experience.

PERFORMING

Using the previously suggested attitude of realizing that there are no auditions, only performances, imagine the additional practice you'll get as a performer.

In actuality, auditions, callbacks, and filming are really variations of the same thing; you act and perform for the videotape camera and the person who's running the commercial session.

You act and perform for the director and clients on the callback. You act and perform for the all of the above plus camera and crew on the actual commercial shoot.

You do the same thing, first for the casting director, then for the show's director and producers, and finally for camera and crew when shooting TV series or features.

Use these opportunities to hone your performing skills. You can either make it work for you or not. The choice is yours.

ACTING AND SET AWARENESS

One of the most awkward aspects of starting a film career is getting used to acting in a film set. All of your acting lessons have been onstage, as has all of your high school, college, and summer-stock experience.

There are no lessons on how to deal with the camera, the set, the crew, shooting out of sequence, protocol, or basically anything to do with the technicalities of filming that the film actor must deal with. Very few opportunities are available to learn these skills, yet actors are expected to know all of these things as soon as they set foot on the set.

Actually, it was this very inequity that prompted me to write my first book, *Hitting Your Mark: What Every Actor Really Needs to Know on a Hollywood Set.*

That book goes a long way toward letting new film actors know what will be expected of them—and how to make it work for them.

The other way to learn it all, of course, is to do it. Commercials are usually an actor's first experience on a film set. Take advantage of this opportunity! Pay very close attention to what's going on around you and why.

The commercial film set is run exactly like the set of an episodic TV show or the most expensive feature made. By getting comfortable working on a commercial film set, you will find yourself rapidly feeling at home as you do your first movie or guest-star role on TV.

WORKING WITH THE DIRECTOR AND CREW

The commercial director is a bit different from the directors you've worked with on your various stage productions. Actually, they do generally the same thing; it's just that film and tape are different mediums.

Directors will still give you your blocking, your motivation, and work with you to perfect your performance and delivery.

Working with film and tape can get highly technical, and the director is everybody's boss. He instructs the camera crew as to what type of setup he wants and what shots to get while in that setup. Then he instructs the lighting crew as to how he wants everything lit. He has to see all the possibilities of how the footage can be edited so he will be able to supply the editor with enough good film to work with.

The commercial director does all of these things, but he also has between two and twenty clients and ad-agency reps looking over his shoulder, second-guessing everything he does.

He's got his hands full. He has a lot of responsibility and a lot of pressure. Some handle it better than others. The more you work with film directors (even in commercials), the more you'll be able to anticipate their needs and wants, thereby making their job of directing you much easier. They like that.

Trying to rehearse while surrounded by cameras, lighting crews, and grips climbing all over the set, laying track, pulling cables, setting up light stands, flags, and gels may at first seem an insurmountable task. As you get used to it, you will incorporate your fourth wall with them as effectively as you do shutting out the audience in a play.

You'll get to the point where, half the time, you won't even be aware of Makeup coming into the set and patting you down, or of Wardrobe adjusting your suit coat.

That kind of familiarity allows you to concentrate more completely on your performance, and it comes only with practice. Filming commercials can give you that experience.

COMPETING

Since we had a chapter devoted to competition, there's no need to add much here except to point out that competing is a skill, and like most skills it becomes easier with practice.

Auditioning for commercials is the perfect place to work on this ability. Here, you will get an opportunity to see what works and what doesn't, what people respond to and what they don't. Ideally, you'll get a handle on these things before your series is on the line.

NETWORKING

If you're new to the business, this may be your introduction to show-biz networking. If you don't have an agent, you'll probably get your first one through introductions and recommendations from friends, acquaintances, or people you've been working with.

Never underestimate the importance of relationships. The more people you can get to know in and around the industry, the better. Everybody knows somebody, and, as an old agent of mine used to say, "You can never tell when the dog may bring home a bone with some *meat* on it!"

FILM FEEDBACK

Like the first time you ever heard your voice recorded and played back, you're likely to recoil in horror the first time you see yourself acting on film. What you intended to do may not be what came across at all.

You may find that you blinked your eyes a lot, or slurred your speech, or that the cool expression you'd come up with actually made you look like a nerd.

Seeing how you come across on film is a good thing to do as soon as possible. Commercials provide excellent opportunities for this type of discovery. Making positive changes not only will help considerably in your theatrical aspirations, but will also make you better at doing commercials.

GETTING DISCOVERED

Any time you work and your face and ability are out there for the public to see, there's always the chance that someone will see you and say, "Get me that person. They're exactly what I need!"

I mentioned earlier just a very few of the stars who began their careers acting in commercials. Another perfect example of what can happen is Courtney Cox. Just think, we may never have known her if she hadn't gotten that little nonspeaking part dancing with Bruce Springsteen in his "Dancing in the Dark" music video.

That, of course, is an extreme case. Two days after that video was released, every guy in the country wanted to know who she was.

Usually, being discovered comes not from who sees you but the people you are working with, and it comes in steps, not all at once. My own story is different.

I was fresh out of college and living in Colorado when it was decided that the 1965 Plymouth commercials would be shot in the Rockies. I was one of many young people hired in Colorado for the job. I also played guitar and wrote some simple little thing that I could sing so that they wouldn't have to pay royalties to anyone.

At the end of practically the first week of shooting, the director, Don Klune, asked what I was doing in Colorado. He said I was perfect for a number of things going on in Hollywood at the time, including the show for which he was currently first assistant director, *Mr. Novak*. This was a series about a high school teacher, and it was shot at MGM. (Even though I was twenty-two, I had always looked young for my age. He thought I'd be just right for one of the high school students.)

I took him at his word, drove to LA with a buddy of mine, met the folks at MGM, and started filming my first episode of *Mr. Novak* three days later.

Now, this doesn't happen often, but I relate it here to show you that it can—and does—happen.

I then attended the MGM contract school (which was winding down). Through my contacts there I got my first agent, which led to my going under contract to Universal (which was just gearing up) and started me off on what has been a most enjoyable career.

And it all started with a commercial filmed in Denver, Colorado.

Stay open, stay positive, and do good work. You can never tell where it all may lead.

IT'S A WRAP

When you are setting out to build a career in commercials, you should realize that no two careers are alike. What you're building will be totally yours, totally unique. It's still good to learn (and borrow) from people you look upon as role models. ("I wish I had a career like that!") There's no problem doing that. Go for it! What's going to happen is that you'll end up creating your own thing anyway.

You are you, the opportunities and situations that exist now are different from the way they were at any other time, as are clients and the casting people involved. The way you progress in this business will be yours alone. Along with this freedom and individuality comes the responsibility to keep it all going.

You are self-employed. Your agents will call with interviews, but what happens then is up to you. It's also up to you to decide what to do when interviews don't come in.

The life of the freelance actor is one of the most unstructured occupations in the world. We seldom know for certain what we're going to be doing from day to day, and we don't have a clue as to what we'll be doing next week. For easy, extemporaneous, spur-of-the-moment kinds of people, it's great.

If you happen to be the type of person who requires a lot of structure or is happiest when you know exactly what's going to be happening on a daily basis, you might want to reconsider your choice of acting as a career.

Commercials run in cycles. Some months are very busy. Others are dead. You'll bounce back and forth from having five interviews in one day to having one in a week. It's good to have something else in your life as well.

For me, it's been writing and sports. I play tennis, golf, and ski whenever I get the chance, and the book you're reading is evidence of the time I devote to writing (which takes a lot of time). I work the above pursuits around my interviews and shoot dates and find that it all fits perfectly. (Also, like many commercial actors, I also still work theatrically in TV, films, and stage, so we factor in those auditions and shoot dates also.) It's important to have a good, healthy mix of work and play in your life.

Personally, I like the free time and think I'd be bored to death doing the same thing every day. Of course, I've lived like this for nearly forty years. Obviously, it suits me. My friends who have steady eight-to-five jobs think I'm crazy. A lifestyle like mine would drive them nuts.

You should take a good look at yourself and see which side you would fall on. There's certainly no right or wrong. It's all personal preference, but the fact of the matter is that, since you have to be available for interviews at any time, your time will have to be flexible to accommodate them.

Is that kind of a life going to make you happy? How will it affect your loved ones? (At some point their needs should be considered, too, you know.) I'm certainly not trying to talk you out of this life, but I am trying to get you to see it as it is! Knowing the reality of the situation could save you a lot of time. You don't want to make a career choice that's wrong for you.

A good example is a friend of mine who got his college degree in Textile Engineering. After graduation, he worked in the field for three months, hated it, quit, and never went back! Fortunately, he happened to be a very talented musician, so that became his life's work, but it still seemed like a major waste of time, energy, and education. That shouldn't happen to you.

Even unstructured lives have some structure, of course. With me, it's pretty simple. If I have interviews, voice-over recordings, meetings, or filming, they come first. If I don't have any of those (or when I've finished with them), I work on whatever writing projects I currently have going. When I've exhausted my brain after a few hours of that, I go play tennis, golf, or work out.

See? It's definitely a loose structure, but a structure nonetheless. Works for me.

Most actors have their own spin on this. Many of us engage in other unstructured occupations or avocations where we can set our own hours. I can write anytime I want to. Other actors get involved in art, music, real estate, playing the stock market, selling cars, consulting, teaching golf or tennis, and so on.

In the beginning of their careers, young actors sometimes work at night as waitresses or bartenders so that they can be available for interviews during the day. Later on, they may own the restaurant or bar.

*   *   *   *

I hope this book has given you a realistic view of what's involved in this business and also imparted a tip or two that may help you along the way. I sincerely wish you well. This business has been wonderful to me and for me. If you're the type of person who enjoys the things we've been dealing with throughout this book, it may be good for you as well.

If so, I welcome you to join me and the other working professionals in this business.

Please remember, in your life as well as your work, keep flexible, keep learning, keep growing, and keep the fun in it. Hang on to your sense of humor. Life is tough enough, but without humor—well, the prospect is too terrible to even consider.

The very best to you all,

Steve Carlson